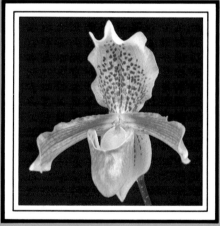

Paphiopedilum insigne

AN ILLUSTRATED GUIDE TO
GROWING YOUR OWN
ORCHIDS

**Easy-to-follow instructions for growing 150
of the world's most beautiful flowers**

Dendrobium nobile

Vanda Rothschildiana

AN ILLUSTRATED GUIDE TO
GROWING YOUR OWN
ORCHIDS

Easy-to-follow instructions for growing 150 of the world's most beautiful flowers

Edited by
Wilma Rittershausen

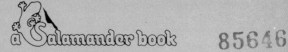

a Salamander book

Published by Arco Publishing, Inc.
NEW YORK

A Salamander Book

Published by Arco Publishing Inc.,
215 Park Avenue South,
New York, N.Y. 10003,
United States of America

© Salamander Books Ltd., 1982
Salamander House,
27 Old Gloucester Street,
London WC1N 3AF,
United Kingdom.

ISBN 0 668 06197 9

Library of Congress Catalog Card
No. 83-83424

All correspondence concerning the
content of this book should be addressed
to Salamander Books Ltd.

Contents

Text and colour photographs are cross-referenced throughout as follows: 64▶

The orchids are arranged in alphabetical order of Latin name. Page numbers in **bold** refer to text entries; those in *italics* refer to photographs.

Credits

Editor/Author: Wilma Ritterhausen is Editor of the *Orchid Review* and the author of several orchid books. She frequently contributes articles to orchid and gardening magazines. Her brother Brian runs the family orchid business set up by their father P R C Rittershausen.

Contributors: Keith Andrew, Ray Bilton, Peter Dumbelton, Alan Greatwood, Paul Phillips and David Stead.

Publisher's editor: Geoff Rogers

Designer: Mark Holt
Photographs: The majority of the photographs have been taken by Eric Crichton. A full list of credits appears on page 160.
Line drawings: David Leigh © Salamander Books Ltd.
Colour reproductions: Scansets Ltd., Rodney Howe Ltd., England.
Monochrome: Bantam Litho Ltd., England
Filmset: SX Composing Ltd., England.

Printed in Belgium by Henri Proost & Cie, Turnhout.

Introduction

The orchid family is one of the largest in the plant kingdom, with at least 25,000 native species around the world. In addition, man has produced over 30,000 hybrids by interbreeding, and more are being produced every year. Most of the wild species found in temperate zones grow as *terrestrial* plants, rooted conventionally in the ground. The majority of cultivated orchids, however, are, or have been bred from, *epiphytic* orchids. These grow on trees or bushes in tropical or subtropical regions, where the climate is sufficiently mild to enable exposed roots to grow. Epiphytes are air plants; they take nothing from their host tree but use it merely as an anchorage. They draw nourishment and water from the air and from humus collected in bark crevices or in the angles of branches. Some epiphytic orchids grow on exposed rocks; these are called *lithophytes*. Generally, epiphytes have the showiest flowers.

Today, far more hybrids are grown than species, many of which have become very rare. The hybrids are usually easier for the beginner to grow successfully because they are vigorous plants able to tolerate the artificial conditions in the greenhouse and home. However, it would be wrong to ignore the beautiful and diverse species, many of which are now raised from seed in nurseries to maintain their populations. Therefore, both hybrids and species are featured in this guide.

Orchid growth patterns

The majority of orchids have a *sympodial* growth pattern. This means that they produce their new growth from the base of previous growths. Most sympodial orchids have *pseudobulbs* – thickened stems adapted to store moisture and food – joined together horizontally by a rhizome. The pseudobulbs vary tremendously in size and shape, as do the leaves they support. The bulbs have a longer life than the leaves, which may be shed after one, two or more seasons. Cymbidiums, cattleyas and odontoglossums are examples of sympodial orchids.

The other basic type of growth seen in orchids is *monopodial*. Here the plant grows from a continually upward growing rhizome, from which pairs of leaves grow at the apex. Vandas and phalaenopsis are examples of monopodials.

The orchid flower

The orchid flower has six segments; an outer ring of three sepals and an inner ring of three petals. The third petal is the *lip* or *labellum*. It serves as a landing platform for the visiting pollinator and is carefully designed to guide it to the pollen contained at the end of the central structure known as the *column*. The pollen is covered by a protective cap and is formed into waxy masses called *pollinia*. After pollination the seed pod develops from the stem immediately behind the flower.

Orchid cultivation

The compost used for orchids should be as close as possible to its natural food source. For this reason the most widely used compost is made up from bark chippings. Bark on its own is a perfectly good medium for all orchids; it is open and well draining and is slow to decompose. For the beginner it is a very easy compost to work with. However, the food supply is restricted and some additional form of feeding will be required. Orchids can be fed in moderation during the spring and summer growing seasons.

Orchids are usually potted in the spring, although young plants are occasionaly potted in the autumn. Repotting will be required every other year. The plants should be kept in pots as small as possible, leaving room after repotting for two years future growth. When potting plants with aerial roots, the roots should be left outside the pot to continue growing. Because of their growth or flowering habits, some orchids are best grown in slatted baskets or on rafts of wood.

Many orchids have a summer growing season followed by a winter resting period. When an orchid is at rest all growth stops and it uses the reserves stored in its pseudobulbs. A resting orchid should be placed in full light and kept mostly dry until the new growth is seen, usually early in the spring. An orchid about to rest may shed some or all of its foliage, depending whether it is an evergreen, deciduous or semi-deciduous type.

Orchids need light, but not bright unshaded sunlight; this will quickly scorch their leaves, particularly in a greenhouse. The glass should be shaded from the early spring to the end of the summer, after which full light should be given to ripen the resting plants.

Orchids can be divided into three temperature ranges. The cool-house varieties require a minimum winter night temperature of 10°C (50°F) rising to a maximum summer day temperature of 24°C (75°F), with an average growing temperature somewhere in between, depending upon the season and immediate weather conditions. The intermediate varieties require a minimum winter night temperature of 13°C (55°F), with a similar growing average and maximum temperature as the cool-house varieties. The warm-house types require no less than 18°C (65°F) as a winter night minimum, and are often better with 21°C (70°F). This should rise by at least 5°C (10°F) during the day. The temperatures quoted at the beginning of the plant descriptions throughout the book are winter night minimums.

While a plant is growing it should be watered freely to maintain an evenly moist condition of the compost, which will maintain the pseudobulbs in a plump state. Humidity should be kept high by damping down the greenhouse or by using humidity trays indoors. Most orchids can be lightly sprayed in summer. Fresh air is also important and should be given at all times.

Propagating orchids
Most orchids can be propagated easily by the amateur. With sympodials the rhizome joining the oldest leafless pseudobulbs can be severed and the bulb potted up on its own. Provided there is a healthy dormant eye, a new growth will appear. The main plant should not be reduced to less than three or four bulbs at any time.

Some monopodial orchids can be propagated by cutting off the top section of the plant, complete with its own root system already growing, and potting it separately. The lower section will often produce new growth. Beginners should wait until they have had success with sympodials before propagating monopodials.

FORKED DEER

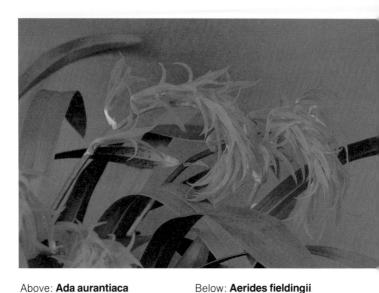

Above: **Ada aurantiaca**
This is a cool-growing species with a compact growth. It blooms in the winter and spring. 17♦

Below: **Aerides fieldingii**
This is an easy species to grow in the intermediate or warm section. Fragrant and spring flowering. 17♦

Above: **Angraecum sesquipedale**
A magnificent species for the warm
greenhouse, where it requires good
light. The large waxy flowers appear
during the winter months. The long
spur extending from the base of the
flower is typical of the whole genus.
The spur may be 30cm (12in) long. 18►

Left: Bifrenaria harrisoniae
An easily grown species for the cool house. It requires good light and flowers during the summer. 20◆

Right: Anguloa clowesii
The large and beautiful cool-growing 'cradle orchid'. Fragrant blooms appear in early summer. 19◆

Below: Angraecum eburneum
A large species for the warm house. Long sprays of fragrant flowers during the winter. 18◆

Far left: **Brassavola digbyana**
Does best in the intermediate section. Likes sun but can be shy flowering. Large, single booms are produced in the summer. 20▸

Below left: **Brassavola nodosa**
This is an intermediate house species that likes the sun. Flowers are freely produced at various times of the year. Beautifully fragrant in the cool of the evening and at night. 21▸

Left: **Brassolaeliocattleya Norman's Bay 'Lows'**
This and similar hybrids are large growers suited to the intermediate greenhouse or warm sunny room indoors. Large fragrant flowers appear in the autumn or spring. 22▸

Below: **Brassia verrucosa**
This cool-house species is a good beginner's orchid. Long sprays of fragrant flowers are produced in the early summer months 21▸

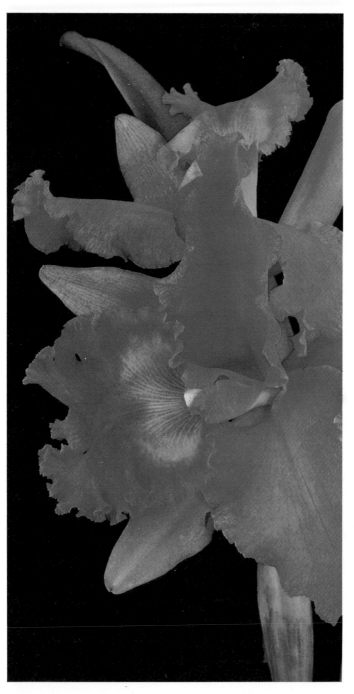

Above:
Brassolaeliocattleya Crusader
This beautiful intermediate-house
hybrid and others like it produce
large fragrant flowers in the spring or
autumn. They can also be grown
indoors. The flowers will last for three
to four weeks on the plant. 22♦

14

Above: **Bulbophyllum collettii**
This extraordinary species can be grown in an intermediate greenhouse. Spring flowering. 23♦

Left: **Cattleya aurantiaca**
One of the smallest of the cattleya species. Cool growing, summer flowering. Very pretty. 24♦

Below: **Calanthe vestita**
A very fine winter-flowering species for the warm greenhouse. Deciduous; blooms while at rest. 23♦

Above: **Cattleya Bow Bells**
*One of the finest of the white-
flowered cattleyas. Very large
fragrant blooms are produced in the
spring. The plant grows quite large
and requires an intermediate
greenhouse or a warm sunny room
to thrive well indoors.* 25▸

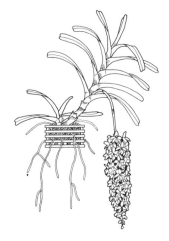

Ada aurantiaca
- Cool: 10°C (50°F)
- Easy to grow and flower
- Winter/spring flowering
- Evergreen/no rest

This species belongs to an extremely small genus of only three species, which are allied to the odontoglossums. It is an epiphyte from Colombia, where it grows in the same location as many of the odontoglossums and therefore requires similar cool house conditions. Although *Ada aurantiaca* is allied to odontoglossums, very little hybridizing has been achieved and the species is grown for its unusually brilliant orange flowers, which appear on compact sprays during the winter and spring. The individual blooms are small and are not fully opening, but produce bell-shaped flowers which are most attractive on the spray.

The plant is a neat, compact grower that can be easily raised from seed and is therefore plentiful. It produces small pseudobulbs, which are partially protected by the base of the outside leaves. The flower spike comes from the base of the leading bulb when it has completed its growth. Pot in an open, well-drained bark compost. Do not overpot. Best when grown on without division. 8♦

Aerides fieldingii
- Intermediate/warm: 13-18°C (55-65°F)
- Easy to grow and flower
- Spring/summer flowering
- Evergreen/semi-dry rest

A popular orchid from tropical Asia. About 50 species have been described. This epiphytic plant grows and flowers well in the intermediate or warm section of the greenhouse. Because it makes many aerial roots, a high degree of humidity is an advantage, with frequent spraying during the summer months.

This is one of the most free-flowering species of the genus, with drooping, branching spikes often up to 60cm (24in) in length. The flowers, which appear in spring or summer, are about 2.5cm (1in) across and are pinky-white suffused and mottled with rose-mauve. This species is also commonly known as the 'foxtail orchid', as are others (for example *Rynchostylis*), that bear their flowers in a similar way. The flowers are sweet-scented, and will remain in perfect condition for up to four weeks if the plant can be kept in cooler conditions while in flower.

Young plants are occasionally produced from the base. These can be removed when ready but ideally the plant should be undisturbed. 8♦

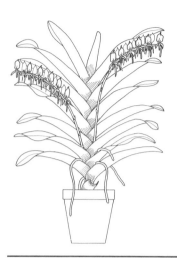

Angraecum eburneum
- **Warm: 18°C (65°F)**
- **Easy to grow and flower**
- **Winter flowering**
- **Evergreen/no rest**

There are over 200 species of angraecums, although very few are seen in cultivation. They come mainly from tropical Africa.

This winter-flowering species resembles *Angraecum sesquipedale* in plant habit but the flower spikes are often longer, producing nine to 12 flowers about 10cm (4in) in diameter. The sepals, petals and spur are green and the lip pure white. Curiously, the flowers appear on the stem as if upside-down.

The plant thrives in generous conditions and should be watered throughout the year. During the summer months regular overhead spraying of the foliage and aerial roots is beneficial. The plant can also be foliar fed in the same way for nine months of the year. Although it likes a position in good light, the leaves are all too easily burnt if it is allowed to stand in bright sunlight for any length of time. A good position for this plant is near to the glass (which should be shaded in summer) suspended in a hanging basket. Not suited to indoor culture. 10♦

Angraecum sesquipedale
- **Warm: 18°C (65°F)**
- **Easy to grow and flower**
- **Winter flowering**
- **Evergreen/no rest**

This is the best-known of the large angraecums and produces one of the most majestic of all orchid flowers. The plant, which can grow to a height of 90cm (36in), has strap-like, leathery leaves that equal the plant's height in span. The star-shaped flowers, produced two to four on stems that arise from the leaf axils, are 15-18cm (6-7in) across and a beautiful creamy-white in colour. Their most distinctive feature is a greenish spur that may be up to 30cm (12in) in length. The flowers appear in the winter months. They are long lasting on the plant and very fragrant.

Even though this epiphytic genus is restricted to parts of Africa and the island of Madagascar, some 200 species are known.

Angraecums are subjects for the warm house, and being without pseudobulbs require moist conditions and plenty of light. However, some of the smaller-growing plants should be protected from full sun, and for all plants frequent spraying can be a great advantage for healthy growth. 9♦

Anguloa clowesii
- **Cool: 11°C (52°F)**
- **Easy to grow and flower**
- **Early summer flowering**
- **Deciduous/rest in winter**

This is a small genus of about ten species, which grow naturally as epiphytes and terrestrials. They are high altitude plants from South America.

This large and beautiful species is commonly known as the 'cradle orchid' owing to the ability of the lip, which is loosely hinged, to rock back and forth when tilted. The lip is fully enclosed by the rest of the flower, which gives rise to a further popular name of 'tulip orchid'. The plant will grow well with lycastes but is considerably larger when in leaf.

Plenty of water and feed should be given during the growing season, when the plant is making up its large pseudobulbs. Water should be withheld when the leaves are shed at the end of the growing season. The flowers, 7.5cm (3in) across, appear singly from a stout stem at the same time as the new growth. They are a lovely canary yellow with a strong fragrance.

This lovely orchid originates from Colombia and today nursery-raised plants are usually available. Suitable for cool greenhouse culture. 11▶

Angulocaste Olympus
- **Cool: 11°C (52°F)**
- **Easy to grow and flower**
- **Spring flowering**
- **Deciduous/rest in winter**

This is a hybrid genus that is the result of crossing *Lycaste* x *Anguloa*. This plant grows and flowers with the ease of its parents and when well grown can become extremely large. It is therefore best suited to a greenhouse where sufficient room can be given.

It should be grown in a good light position with full light during the winter, when it is dormant and becomes deciduous. This plant has a short but fast growing season, when extra artificial feed can be given. When repotting, a small amount of dried cow manure can be incorporated in the base to enrich the compost.

The flowers are large and heavily textured and last for several weeks in the spring and early summer. In form they are midway between those of the two parent genera. The colour can vary considerably from white and cream to yellow. The foliage on this orchid is easily spoiled by water and should therefore not be sprayed from overhead.

Because of its size, this hybrid does not make an ideal house plant.

Bifrenaria harrisoniae
- Cool: 11°C (52°F)
- Easy to grow, shy to flower
- Early summer flowering
- Evergreen/dry rest

This is the most familiar species of
the *Bifrenaria* genus. It produces
creamy-white flowers, one or two to
a stem, with thick waxy sepals and
petals and a lip covered with short,
reddish-purple hairs. Each flower
can be up to 7.5cm (3in) in diameter.

It belongs to a small genus of
about a dozen species, coming
mainly from Brazil. They are certainly
among the easiest of plants to grow,
and are often offered in collections
for beginners.

Although they are usually grown in
the intermediate house, with plenty
of light, they will also do well in the
cool house with a winter minimum of
11°C (52°F). Bifrenarias are
epiphytic and will succeed if grown in
a pot on the staging, or in wire or
wooden baskets suspended from
the roof; in either position they
should be kept drier at the root when
not in active growth. An open
compost with good drainage is
important.

Allow the plant a complete rest
during the winter, giving no water
until the new growth is seen to
appear during the very early spring.
Propagation is a slow process. 10▶

Brassavola digbyana
- Intermediate: 13°C (55°F)
- Challenge to grow and flower
- Summer flowering
- Evergreen/dry rest

This is the largest of the genus
which, though still horticulturally
known as *Brassavola,* is botanically
more correctly *Rhyncholaelia
digbyana.* In commercial catalogues
it can be found under either name.

The lemon-scented flower is
incredibly beautiful and contains a
deep fringe to the lip, which is a rare
occurrence in orchids. The reason
for this deeply fimbriated lip is not
fully understood, although it is
thought to guide or assist the
pollinating insect in some way.
Usually single flowers are produced
which last for up to three weeks.

The plant has been used very
extensively in hybridization to
produce the large-lipped
brassocattleyas etc, although the
distinctive shape of the fringe, so
characteristic of the species, has
never been reproduced to the same
extent in its offspring.

The apex of the intermediate
greenhouse is an ideal position for
this sun-worshipping plant, where it
will thrive in the air movement at the
roof of the house. 12▶

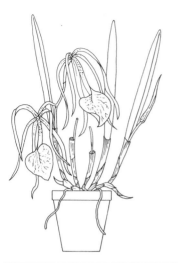 

Brassavola nodosa
- **Intermediate: 13°C (55°F)**
- **Moderately easy to grow**
- **Variable flowering season**
- **Evergreen/dry rest**

Brassavolas are very popular with amateur growers, partly because they are easy to cultivate and also for the strange shapes of some of the flowers. The 15 species known are either epiphytic or lithophytic and come from Central and South America.

In this species the pseudobulbs and leaves are very slender and appear as one, both being cylindrical in shape. The plants are best grown on tree-fern fibre, with just a little compost, and suspended from the greenhouse roof. Brassavolas object to excessive moisture and should be kept quite dry during their lengthy period of rest. They do well in the conditions suitable for cattleyas.

Brassavola nodosa is very fragrant, especially in the cool of the evening or at night. It can be found in flower at any time of the year. The flowers, often four to five on a stem, are creamy-green and up to 7.5cm (3in) across when fully open. The lip is broad, and white with a few purple spots in the throat.

Some hybridization has been done with this species but not on the same scale as *B. digbyana*. 12◆

Brassia verrucosa
- **Cool: 10°C (50°F)**
- **Easy to grow and flower**
- **Early summer flowering**
- **Evergreen/semi-rest**

This is one of the most popular of the brassias, a genus of epiphytic orchids from South America. They are allied to, and will interbreed with, plants from the odontoglossum group. *B. verrucosa* is a neat, compact grower that will do well indoors or in a cool greenhouse. During the winter it requires slightly less water than in the summer months, but it should not be allowed to dry out so that the pseudobulbs shrivel. The sweetly fragrant flowers are carried on graceful sprays of up to a dozen blooms during the early summer. The sepals and petals are curiously long and narrow, which gives rise to the plant's common name of 'spider orchid'. This characteristic gives the flowers a lovely light and wispy appearance. The colour is light green with darker green spotting.

This plant will often 'climb' out of its pot and is a good subject for mounting on wood, when long aerial roots are produced. An ideal orchid for beginners.

Although about 30 species of this genus are known, only a very few are still grown. 13◆

21

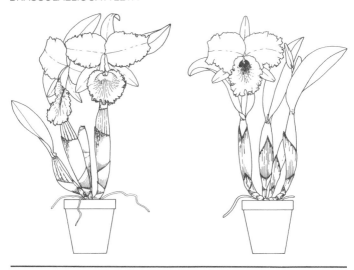

Brassolaeliocattleya Crusader

- **Intermediate: 13°C (55°F)**
- **Easy to grow and flower**
- **Winter flowering**
- **Evergreen/some rest**

This robust hybrid is the result of a cross between *Brassolaeliocattleya* Queen Elizabeth and *Laeliocattleya* Trivanhoe, and requires intermediate temperature conditions. The large pink flowers, produced in winter, are 20-23cm (8-9in) across. The heavy, round lip is purple with a yellow patch inside the lobes.

First raised in 1941, this plant has been a very popular hybrid ever since. It has also produced some excellent offspring that continue the line of rich pink-purple colouring. It is typical of modern hybrids with three separate genera in its pedigree. These are *Brassavola, Laelia* and *Cattleya*. The qualities of all three have combined to give size and colour to the flower. These hybrids can be grown indoors provided they are given extremely good light.

In addition they require some rest after they have flowered in the winter, or until the new growth begins to show. During this rest the pseudobulbs should not be allowed to shrivel extensively. 14◆

Brassolaeliocattleya Norman's Bay 'Lows'
(FCC/RHS)

- **Intermediate: 13°C (55°F)**
- **Easy to grow and flower**
- **Autumn flowering**
- **Evergreen/some rest**

Probably one of the finest rose-magenta flowered hybrids, this plant is a cross of *Brassocattleya* Hartland and *Laeliocattleya* Ishtar. The flowers, which are 20-23cm (8-9in) across, have a splendid frilled lip and a lovely fragrance.

Like all intergeneric cattleyas this plant should be grown in good light and rested for part of the year. This resting period usually follows flowering and so will vary from plant to plant. Some time after flowering the new growths will show signs of activity and at this stage normal watering can be resumed.

Propagation is achieved by severing the rhizome in between the older, leafless bulbs and potting singly, or they may be left in the pot until the propagated bulbs have started independent growths a few weeks later.

These young propagations will require growing on for at least three or four years to attain flowering size. By this time the original bulb will have withered away completely. 13◆

Bulbophyllum collettii
- **Intermediate: 13°C (55°F)**
- **Easy to grow and flower**
- **Spring flowering**
- **Evergreen/semi-rest**

Calanthe vestita
- **Warm: 18°C (65°F)**
- **Easy to grow and flower**
- **Winter flowering**
- **Deciduous/dry rest**

Coming from Burma, this is a plant for the intermediate house; it flowers during the spring. It has roundish, angular pseudobulbs spaced well apart on a creeping rhizome. The four to six flowers, produced on a flower spike that appears when the new growth is only partly completed, have lower sepals that hang down, as if joined, to a length of 13cm (5in). The top sepal and petals carry tufts of short, fine hairs that flutter in even a slight air movement. The overall flower colour is maroon-red with yellow stripes.

This plant is not deeply rooted, and does best in shallow pots or on tree fern or cork bark. Good drainage is essential.

Not only are bulbophyllums widely distributed throughout the subtropical and tropical areas of the world, but their vegetative growth habit and flower size and shape are also equally varied.

They comprise the largest genus in the orchid family, containing about 2000 species. The majority of these are highly botanical. 15♦

With tall, upright flower spikes and many long-lasting flowers, *Calanthe* is deservedly a special favourite with orchid growers. Given warm-house conditions, it grows easily and is thus a good plant for beginners. Of the 150 species known, most are terrestrials; they come from a wide area, including South Africa, Asia and Central America.

The flowers of *Calanthe vestita* range in colour from white to deep pink, the lip often being stronger in colour than the rest of the flower.

A warm greenhouse with good light suits this plant best. This deciduous species produces rather large, angular pseudobulbs with wide, ribbed leaves. During the growing season the plant should be liberally watered and fed until the leaves turn yellow and fall during the early winter months. At this stage watering should be gradually reduced. After flowering the pseudobulbs should be repotted in a well-drained compost with the addition of a little dried cow manure in the base. 15♦

Catasetum pileatum
- **Intermediate: 13°C (55°F)**
- **Moderately easy to grow**
- **Autumn flowering**
- **Deciduous/dry rest**

Cattleya aurantiaca
- **Cool: 11°C (52°F)**
- **Easy to grow and flower**
- **Summer flowering**
- **Evergreen/slight rest**

This species belongs to a very strange and interesting genus of Central American orchids, whose flowers are handsomely curious rather than beautiful. Stout pseudobulbs are produced with papery leaves that last for one season only and are discarded by the plant at the end of its growing period, usually about the time of flowering. During the winter the plant is resting and should be given no water until after the new growth has started in the spring. It is quite rare in cultivation but nursery-raised plants are sometimes available.

The curious flowers can vary tremendously in colour, from almost white to deep red in some varieties. The flower has an extraordinary mechanism that enables the pollen to be ejected from the flower when the sensitive parts are touched. The lip is very large and shaped like a half cup. Another curious feature is the thick mat of short, stiff aerial roots often seen at its base. The flower is intensely fragrant and can be up to 18cm (7in) across.

This small bifoliate species comes from Guatemala and neighbouring countries. It has drooping clusters of red-orange flowers, 7.5-10cm (3-4in) across, produced in summer. The plant is peculiar in that it produces seedpods by self-pollination, which means that often the flowers do not open properly and the prettiness of the flowers is lost. Today plants are raised from selected nursery stock that produces fully opening flowers.

This species is one of the smallest growing and flowering varieties of *Cattleya* in cultivation. The plant will flower when only 15cm (6in) tall and is therefore easily accommodated in a small greenhouse or indoor growing case. Because of its diminutive pseudobulbs, *Cattleya aurantiaca* should not be allowed to remain in a dry state for any prolonged period. It is at its best when grown on into a large mature plant without being divided. 15▶

Cattleya Bow Bells

- Intermediate: 13°C (55°F)
- Easy to grow and flower
- Spring flowering
- Evergreen/some rest

One of the world's most famous cattleyas, this beautiful hybrid has been bred from the cross of *C.* Edithae and *C.* Suzanne Hye. It produces large heavy flowers, 15cm (6in) across, with pure white overlapping petals and a sulphur-yellow mark in the back of the throat. It is a plant for the intermediate house and requires a rest during the winter after the new growth has matured. The flowers are produced in the spring.

Where this and other *Cattleya* hybrids are grown together the flowering season can be extended through the autumn and winter months well into the spring and early summer. The colours available vary from deep lavenders and pinks through to pure white. The glistening sepals and petals of the white cattleyas are among the purest colour to be found in orchids. To encourage the blooms to last longer in perfection the plants should be kept dry while in flower.

Cattleyas such as this provide the largest of flowers cultivated. 16♦

Cattleya bowringiana

- Intermediate: 11-13°C (52-55°F)
- Easy to grow and flower
- Autumn flowering
- Evergreen/winter rest

This highly productive plant can produce as many as 20 rose-purple blooms, 7.5cm (3in) across, with a deep purple lip, marked with golden yellow in the throat. It requires more water than most to support the long pseudobulbs, which are slightly bulbous at the base. The flowers open during late autumn, and the plant benefits from a short mid-winter rest after flowering, during which time watering should be withheld.

This is an excellent plant for a beginner, although it is now becoming increasingly difficult to obtain. The plant is slow growing from seed, and is not therefore readily available as nursery-raised stock. However, it can be grown and propagated with ease, so it is worth looking out for. Like all cattleyas it prefers a well-drained compost and is intolerant of soggy conditions.

This species originates from Guatemala and grows epiphytically in the wild. Some very interesting hybrids have been raised from it since its introduction in 1884. 33♦

Cattleya forbesii

- ● **Intermediate: 13°C (55°F)**
- ● **Easy to grow and flower**
- ● **Late summer flowering**
- ● **Evergreen/semi-rest**

Discovered in Brazil in 1823, this plant is a bifoliate of dainty growth, with pencil-thin pseudobulbs. Its yellow or tan-coloured flowers, produced in summer, are 7.5-10cm (3-4in) across, and have a tubular lip with side lobes of pale pink on the outside, and a deep yellow throat marked with wavy red lines.

This is an easy plant for the beginner and is also suitable for culture in an indoor growing case. It should not be overpotted, but kept in as small a pot as possible; unlike many cattleyas it rarely becomes top heavy. It should be grown in a position of good light all the year round and during the summer months can be lightly sprayed with water, taking care to avoid the flowers while in bloom. At one time this plant was considered a rather insignificant member of the genus, but today its smaller, pastel flowers are welcomed as charming and delicate.

This species has been little used for hybridizing. The plant can be propagated by careful division when large enough. 33♦

Chysis bractescens

- ● **Cool/Intermediate:**
  10-13°C (50-55°F)
- ● **Fairly easy to grow**
- ● **Early summer flowering**
- ● **Semi-deciduous/dry rest**

The flowers of this species, up to 7.5cm (3in) in diameter, grow rather close together on a single but comparatively short stem produced from new growth. They are white, turning to cream with age; the lip is white on the outer surface and tinged with yellow inside.

The six species of *Chysis* recorded, which come mainly from Mexico, are all epiphytic and semi-deciduous under cultivation. When in growth the plants require a liberal supply of heat and moisture; when they have shed their leaves they should be transferred to the cool house for a period of rest. During this time they should be kept much drier at the root until growth restarts in the spring.

Growth and form are similar in all the species. A few, often large, leaves grow from the upper half of the spindle-shaped pseudobulbs, which may be up to 46cm (18in) long. These either grow horizontally or hang down, so that the plants are best grown in baskets.

Repot every other year using a well-draining compost.

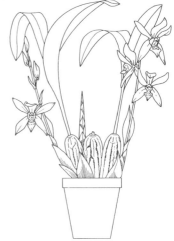

Coelogyne cristata

- Cool: 10°C (50°F)
- Challenge to flower
- Winter/spring flowering
- Evergreen/dry rest

Perhaps the most familiar of the genus, this species likes to grow on undisturbed into a specimen plant. The flower spike appears from the centre of the new growth and its snowy-white flowers, broken only by a blotch of golden yellow at the centre of the lip, appear in mid-winter and last for four or five weeks.

Although the genus contains well over 100 species, few coelogynes are found in collections today. This is a pity, for they are orchids of great merit. They are, in the main, easy to grow and many species thrive in cool conditions, requiring a warmer environment only during their active growing season. Rest well in winter to achieve flowering.

Many coelogynes are suitable for growing on into specimen plants. However, be warned: a specimen plant of one of the larger-growing species can take up a considerable amount of space in the greenhouse. Fortunately, it is possible to choose from a wide range of smaller-growing species, and even a single-growth plant in flower is a valuable addition to any orchid collection. 33♦

Coelogyne ochracea

- Cool: 10°C (50°F)
- Easy to grow and flower
- Early summer flowering
- Evergreen/dry rest

This popular species from India has shiny green pseudobulbs topped by a pair of leaves. The flower spikes are produced freely from the new growth while it is very young. Like all coelogynes, it prefers to be grown on into a specimen plant with as little disturbance as possible, although this species is unlikely to become unmanageable in size. The flowers are extremely pretty and full of fragrance.

After flowering grow the plant on well into the autumn, by which time the season's growth will have matured and the plant will rest. Place in full light for the winter and withhold all water until the new growths appear in early spring. The pseudobulbs will shrivel during this time but they will quickly plump up again when normal watering is resumed.

Ideal for beginners, it is equally at home indoors or in a cool greenhouse. The most frequent mistake made is watering while the plant is resting in the winter, when it must be kept dry at the roots. Repot when necessary after flowering. 34♦

Coelogyne pandurata
- **Intermediate/warm: 16°C (60°F)**
- **Fairly easy to grow**
- **Summer flowering**
- **Evergreen/dry rest**

Colax jugosus
- **Intermediate: 13°C (55°F)**
- **Fairly easy to grow and flower**
- **Spring flowering**
- **Evergreen/semi-dry rest**

The fragrant flowers of this species can be up to 10cm (4in) across and are among the largest of all coelogynes. They are green with jet black hairs partly covering the lip and are borne in beautiful arching sprays that appear from the centre of the new growth.

The species originates from Borneo and therefore likes warmer conditions than the cool growing Indian species. It should only be attempted where sufficient room can be provided for it. The large pseudobulbs are spaced well apart along a creeping rhizome and for this reason the plant can be more easily accommodated in a boat-shaped basket or box rather than a round pot. A complete rest during the winter is vital for successful flowering.

The old pseudobulbs may be used for propagation provided their removal does not weaken the main plant. This orchid is not widely available.

Repot every other year, using a compost of coarse bark. Repot when the new growth appears. 35♦

Native to Brazil, this species grows well in intermediate conditions with plenty of fresh air. The plant can easily be accommodated in a small greenhouse, for it seldom grows above 30cm (12in) in height. It seems to do best when kept fairly potbound, but the compost must be of an open nature to give good drainage.

The plant develops small oval pseudobulbs, 2.5-5cm (1-2in) in height, narrowing towards the top, and two dark green leaves 15-23cm (6-9in) long. The flowers, often two but sometimes three to a spike, are about 5cm (2in) in diameter. The sepals and petals are creamy-white, the sepals being clear and the petals heavily blotched with deep purple; the lip is similarly marked. The plant flowers in spring and early summer.

The three species of *Colax* have in the past been included in the genera *Lycaste, Maxillaria* and *Zygopetalum,* but are now accepted as a separate genus, *Pabista.* However, the accepted name remains *Colax.* 35♦

Cymbidiella rhodochila

- **Warm: 18°C (65°F)**
- **A challenge to grow**
- **Winter/spring flowering**
- **Evergreen/no rest**

This is an epiphytic plant that produces similar growth to that of a cymbidium, but has generally shorter leaves. The flowers – and there can be none more striking – are produced from winter to spring on a stem arising from the base of the pseudobulb. There can be as many as 20, which open in succession, three or four at any one time. Each flower measures about 7.5cm (3in) across and, being of heavy texture, they are long-lasting. The sepals and slightly hooded petals are yellowish-green, the latter thickly spotted with dark green; the lip, in contrast, is crimson, with some yellow and dark green spots in the centre.

   Cymbidiellas are subjects for the warm house, provided with an abundance of moisture and good light, though not direct sunshine.

   Only three species of this most attractive orchid are known, all native to Madagascar, and only *Cymbidiella rhodochila* is likely to be found in collections today. At first the genus was linked with *Cymbidium,* but it is now accepted as separate. 35♦

Cymbidium Angelica 'Advent'

(AM/RHS)
- **Cool: 10°C (50°F)**
- **Easy to grow and flower**
- **Autumn/winter flowering**
- **Evergreen/no rest**

This superb autumn to winter flowering yellow hybrid (*Cym.* Lucy Moor x *Cym.* Lucense) is fast becoming a very famous breeding plant and is being used by cymbidium hybridists throughout the world. Up to 14 large flowers, 13cm (5in) across, are carried on upright spikes. The petals and sepals are pale yellow and the cream-coloured lip is lightly spotted with dark red, the spotting becoming dense in the throat.

   Cymbidium hybrids can become considerably large, and are best suited to a greenhouse where sufficient room can be given them. Overhead spraying is particularly beneficial during the summer growing season. If grown too warm without the cool night temperature recommended, the plants are unlikely to flower the following season. This is one of the earliest of the top class cymbidiums to bloom, and with careful selection of varieties the season can exceed six months. This very attractive cymbidium deserves a place in every collection. 36♦

Cymbidium Ayres Rock 'Cooksbridge Velvet'
- Cool: 10°C (50°F)
- Easy to grow and flower
- Winter/spring flowering
- Evergreen/no rest

One of a new generation of cymbidiums in which the colour range has been extended even further towards the deeper pinks. The flowers, 11cm (4.25in) across, are crimson tinged with white and the lip is a rich dark crimson, boldly edged with white.

A supporting cane will be required by most of these *Cymbidium* hybrids to prevent the heavy flower spikes snapping or buckling under their own weight as they develop. Though these flowers will last eight or ten weeks on the plant, it is advisable (particularly with young plants) to remove the spike after the last flower has been open for about ten days. This reduces the strain on the plant at a time when new growths are appearing. The cut spike of flowers will last just as long in water in a cool room indoors.

This is one of the easiest orchids to propagate. The old leafless pseudobulbs can be removed from the plant at repotting time and potted singly. 37♦

Cymbidium Bulbarrow 'Our Midge'
- Cool: 10°C (50°F)
- Easy to grow and flower
- Late spring flowering
- Evergreen/no rest

The Bulbarrow hybrids have rightly gained a reputation throughout the world. The crossing of the standard Western Rose with the miniature species, *Cym. devonianum,* has resulted in some excellent clones, most of which have flowers with very fine lips of striking colours.

'Our Midge' bears spikes of up to 20 flowers in late spring. The 2.5-4cm (1-1.5in) flowers are soft rose-red with deep crimson lips.

The miniature hybrid cymbidiums provide an alternative for the grower with limited space. Being smaller and more easily managed plants, they can be accommodated in the home. Their more compact blooms are just as rewarding, and are often of rich colouring where the species *Cymbidium devonianum* has been used as a parent.

Cymbidiums, particularly if grown in the drier indoor atmosphere, can be prone to attacks from red spider mite. Regular sponging and wiping of the leaves with water, particularly the undersides, will keep this at bay. 36♦

Cymbidium devonianum

- Cool: 10°C (50°F)
- Easy to grow and flower
- Spring flowering
- Evergreen/semi-dry rest

This miniature species originates from the Himalayas and has been used often in breeding miniatures. The flowers, borne on pendent spikes, normally open in late spring and early summer. They are basically green speckled with red, and the triangular lip is clouded with purple. When the flower spikes first appear they have the annoying habit of burrowing into the compost. A label should be placed under the spikes to ensure that they grow horizontally towards the rim of the pot.

This species differs in its appearance from the conventional cymbidium. The pseudobulbs are small, but the leaves are considerably wider, narrowing sharply towards the base. Unlike most cymbidiums, this species requires a semi-rest during the winter, with only occasional watering.

This plant, once extremely common in cultivation, is rapidly becoming a rarity. 36♦

Cymbidium Dingwall 'Lewes'

- Cool: 10°C (50°F)
- Easy to grow and flower
- Late spring flowering
- Evergreen/no rest

A hybrid resulting from a cross between *Cym.* Pearl Easter and *Cym.* Merlin. Pearl Easter is a superb parent for producing flowers with clear white sepals and petals and the combination with Merlin has produced some very fine late spring flowering whites. This plant is free-flowering and bears up to 12 large 13cm (5in) flowers on an upright spike. The petals and sepals are white and the lip is marked with red.

Young plants will bloom on one flower spike from the leading growth. As the plant matures more than one new growth will be made each season. Each new growth can be capable of flowering, so the number of flower spikes on a large plant is directly related to the number of new growths. Nothing looks finer than a large plant with six or more flowering spikes, although to achieve this standard without dividing the plant, adequate room must be available. While flowering, the plants should be kept well shaded to prevent discolouration by the sun. 37♦

Cymbidium eburneum

- Cool: 10°C (50°F)
- A challenge to flower
- Winter/spring flowering
- Evergreen/no rest

Discovered in the 1830s by the botanical explorer William Griffiths, this species is native to the Khasia hills in northern India. It is a compact grower with narrow pseudobulbs, and leaves that can grow to more than 60cm (24in) in length. The erect flower spike arises higher up on the bulb than in most cymbidiums, and several spikes are often carried at the same time. The plant is often erratic in its flowering, producing from one to three 7.5cm (3in) flowers to each spike. The flowers, which open in winter and early spring, are white to ivory in colour, with a deep yellow band in the middle of the lip, flanked by two yellow keels.

Very prominent in hybridization, *Cym. eburneum* was one of the parents of the first hybrid cymbidium to be raised in cultivation – Eburneolowianum – which was registered by Veitch in 1889. Although it is an important species in breeding, the plant does not grow vigorously, and is a shy bloomer. It is now rare and considered a collector's item.38♦

Cymbidium Fort George 'Lewes'
(AM/RHS)

- Cool: 10°C (50°F)
- Easy to grow and flower
- Winter/spring flowering
- Evergreen/no rest

One of the finest free-flowering, green-coloured cymbidiums in the world, often giving two spikes per bulb with up to 14 flowers per spike on an upright stem. The flowers are up to 12cm (4.75in) in diameter. The bringing together of two of the most famous green-flowered parents (*Cym.* Baltic x *Cym.* York Meradith) has produced an excellent result.

To achieve regular flowering all cymbidiums should be repotted every other year, keeping them as large as can be managed. They can be fed throughout almost the whole year, reducing both feed and water to a minimum during the shortest days for three months of the year.

The blooms of cymbidiums are highly in demand as cut flowers and are certainly more popular with florists than any other orchid bloom. For this purpose they can be grown in large beds, where they grow exceedingly well, producing even more vigorous plants than those raised individually in pots in the accepted way. 39♦

Above: **Cattleya forbesii**
One of the smaller Cattleya *species.
It blooms in late summer and is ideal
for beginners.* 26♦

Right: **Coelogyne cristata**
*A delightful cool-house species that
must be rested well to flower
regularly. Spring blooming.* 27♦

Below: **Cattleya bowringiana**
*Grows in the intermediate house and
flowers in the autumn. Large heads
of attractive flowers.* 25♦

Above: **Coelogyne ochracea**
*One of the prettiest and easiest
orchids to grow. Ideal for a beginner,
in a cool greenhouse or indoors. A
compact grower that blooms freely in
the spring, with sprays of dainty,
fragrant, white and yellow blooms.
Very pretty. Keep dry in winter.* 27♦

Above: **Coelogyne pandurata**
*This lovely, summer-flowering,
fragrant species likes conditions in
the warm greenhouse.* 28◗

Right: **Cymbidiella rhodochila**
*An unusual species suitable for the
warm house, where it blooms during
the winter and spring.* 29◗

Below: **Colax jugosus**
*This beautiful intermediate species
is not often seen. It blooms during
the spring.* 28◗

Above: **Cymbidium Bulbarrow 'Our Midge'**
A superb miniature hybrid to bloom in the late spring. 30♦

Above:
Cymbidium Angelica 'Advent'
One of the finest varieties for autumn and winter flowers. Cool growing. An easy beginner's orchid. 29♦

Below: **Cymbidium devonianum**
An ideal beginner's orchid. Cool growing and spring flowering. Flower spikes hang downwards. Needs a semi-rest during the winter. 31♦

Above: **Cymbidium Ayres Rock 'Cooksbridge Velvet'**
A fine dark-flowered hybrid. Spring flowering. Cool growing. The flowers will last up to 10 weeks. 30♦

Below:
Cymbidium Dingwall 'Lewes'
A fine white hybrid for late spring flowering. An easy-to-grow, cool-house variety. 31♦

Above: **Cymbidium eburneum**
*This cool-growing species produces
one to three flowers in the winter and
spring months.* 32♦

Left: **Cymbidium lowianum**
*Long, arching sprays are produced
by this lovely, cool-growing, spring-
flowering species.* 49♦

Above right:
Cymbidium Fort George 'Lewes'
*A cool-growing hybrid for winter/
spring flowers. Upright spikes.* 32♦

Right: **Cymbidium Stonehaven
'Cooksbridge'**
*A many-flowered miniature variety to
bloom in the autumn and winter.* 50♦

Above: **Cymbidium traceyanum**
A strongly scented species that blooms in the autumn. Cool growing. Long sprays of flowers are produced. Many hybrids are available from this species, which is now considered to be a collector's item in some parts of the world. 51♦

Below:
Cymbidium Touchstone 'Janis'
This is a beautiful miniature hybrid that carries semi-pendent spikes in the winter and spring. Ideal for beginners, it has a compact habit and is cool growing. 50♦

Above: **Dendrobium aureum**
*An easy-to-grow, cool, compact
species that is ideal for the beginner.
Flowers in the early spring.* 51♦

Left: **Dendrobium Fiftieth State**
*A warm-growing hybrid that blooms
in the summer sunshine. Very long-
lasting flowers.* 52♦

Above: **Dendrobium densiflorum**
*One of the most beautiful of the
spring-flowering species. Dense,
golden yellow trusses are freely*
*produced in the spring after resting.
The plant is cool growing and keeps
its leaves all winter. Becoming
scarce in cultivation.* 52♦

Above:
Dendrobium Gatton Sunray
This is a massive grower that needs plenty of room in the intermediate *greenhouse. Its highly decorative blooms are produced during the summer in pendent trusses. The flowers may be 10cm (4in) across.* 53▶

Left: **Dendrobium infundibulum**
One of the showiest Dendrobium species. Cool growing. Several large flowers are produced at the top of the bulb during the spring. 53♦

Right: **Dendrobium Louisae**
A warm-growing, sun-loving hybrid for autumn/winter blooming. Produces long sprays of flowers that are very long lasting. 54♦

Below: **Dendrobium nobile**
A very popular, cool-growing species that blooms in the spring. It flowers the entire length of the bulb. Requires good light. 54♦

Below right: **Dendrobium pierardii**
An extremely tall-growing species for the intermediate house, best grown downwards. Flowers the length of the bulb. Deciduous. 55♦

Far left: **Dendrobium Tangerine 'Tillgates'**
An unusual hybrid for the intermediate house. 57♦

Left: **Dendrobium superbum**
A large-flowered, highly fragrant species for the intermediate house. Spring flowering, deciduous. 56♦

Below left:
Dendrobium speciosum
An unusual species that flowers in the spring. Fragrant blooms. 56♦

Right: **Dendrobium secundum**
Dense clusters of small, attractive flowers in spring and summer. An evergreen variety for the intermediate house. 55♦

Below: **Dendrobium transparens**
A fragrant species for intermediate conditions. Flowers the length of the bulb in the spring. Tall, slender deciduous bulbs. 57♦

Above: **Dendrobium wardianum**
A cool-growing species that blooms early in the year. Flowers the length of the bulb. 58♦

Above right:
Dendrobium williamsonii
Compact-growing, fragrant species for the cool house. Summer. 58♦

Right: **Doritis pulcherrima**
An attractive warm-house species with tall, upright spikes. Treat as Phalaenopsis *for success.* 59♦

Below: **Dracula chimaera**
Formerly Masdevallia. *Unusual cool-house species. Winter to spring flowering. Single flowers.* 60♦

Above: **Encyclia cochleata**
This is a very popular cool-house
species suitable for beginners.
Flowers in succession, producing
months of blooms at various times of
the year. A compact grower, it also
does well indoors. Called the
'cockleshell orchid'. 6161♦

Cymbidium lowianum
- ● **Cool: 10°C (50°F)**
- ● **Easy to grow and flower**
- ● **Late spring flowering**
- ● **Evergreen/no rest**

Discovered in 1887 in upper Burma, and also found in Thailand, this species has exerted its influence in almost all of our modern hybrids. The plant, which flowers in late spring, normally carries very large arching sprays of green flowers, up to 10cm (4in) across, with a V-shaped red mark on the lip. There is also the variety *concolor*, which has a yellow marking on the lip.

   The plant conforms in appearance to the typical cymbidium, but it is easily identified when not in flower by the slender shape of its pseudobulbs. At one time extremely common, it lost its popularity to the numerous hybrids it helped to create. Now it is unobtainable from its native home; plants are nursery-raised in limited numbers to meet the new demand as growers rediscover this lovely species.

   The plant may be quite easily propagated by the removal of the leafless pseudobulbs. To maintain a plant of flowering size, it should not be reduced to less than four or five bulbs. 38♦

Cymbidium Peter Pan 'Greensleeves'
- ● **Cool: 10°C (50°F)**
- ● **Easy to grow and flower**
- ● **Autumn flowering**
- ● **Evergreen/no rest**

One of the most popular of the autumn flowering varieties, this plant will grow equally well indoors or in a greenhouse. Its compact habit enables it to be grown into a large specimen plant without division, when several flower spikes will be produced in a season. The flowers are a little over 7.5cm (3in) across. The petals and sepals are soft green, and the lip is heavily marked and edged with deep crimson. Do not allow the flowers to remain on the plant for too long. After two weeks they should be removed and placed in water.

   This is a fine example of a hybrid that has inherited the best characteristics from both its parents (*Cym. ensifolium* x *Cym.* Miretta). From *Cym. ensifolium* the plant has inherited its autumn flowering habit together with a beautiful fragrance, and Miretta has greatly enhanced the quality of the flower.

   Repotting, when necessary, should be done in the spring. Surplus leafless pseudobulbs can be removed and used for propagation.

Cymbidium Stonehaven 'Cooksbridge'

- Cool: 10°C (50°F)
- Easy to grow and flower
- Autumn/winter flowering
- Evergreen/no rest

This second generation *Cym. pumilum* hybrid (*Cym.* Putana x *Cym.* Cariga) is a very good quality, medium-sized plant that produces strong spikes with up to 25 fine , 7cm (2.75in) flowers. Opening in autumn and early winter, the flowers are cream-coloured and the lip is pale yellow, edged with dark red. The plant is very free-flowering and easy to grow. Such plants are becoming increasingly popular as pot plants for the home.

While the flower spikes are developing, some support will be required. A thin bamboo cane should be inserted close to the spike and tied into position. The developing buds should not be supported until they are well developed, or the supporting ties must be adjusted almost daily as the spike grows. If the recommended night-time temperature cannot be kept down, the plant will be reluctant to bloom. During the summer such plants can be grown out of doors while temperatures permit. 39♦

Cymbidium Touchstone 'Janis'

- Cool: 10°C (50°F)
- Easy to grow and flower
- Winter/spring flowering
- Evergreen/no rest

This miniature variety is another fine example of *Cym. devonianum* breeding (*Cym. devonianum* x Mission Bay). The plants from this crossing are small and free growing, and produce beautiful arching sprays of flowers during the winter and early spring. The flowers are bronze with contrasting deep crimson lips and are 2.5-4cm (1-1.5in) across.

An ideal beginner's plant for indoor or greenhouse culture. It should be kept watered throughout the year, never being allowed to dry out completely. During the spring, summer and autumn months the plant should be lightly fed. Cool night-time temperatures are important for successful flowering. Repotting will be necessary every other year. This should be done immediately after flowering and using a size larger pot. If there are too many leafless pseudobulbs, some should be removed to restore the balance of the plant. Water should be witheld for a few days after repotting is completed. 39♦

Cymbidium traceyanum

- Cool: 10°C (50°F)
- Easy to grow and flower
- Autumn flowering
- Evergreen/no rest

Dendrobium aureum

- Cool: 10°C (50°F)
- Easy to grow and flower
- Early spring flowering
- Deciduous/dry winter rest

This very interesting and flamboyant species was exported in great quantities from Thailand at the beginning of the century. The number collected in the early years resulted in the virtual disappearance of the plant from its natural habitat.

The species is autumn to winter flowering and produces long arching sprays of 10-13cm (4-5in) flowers. The flowers are strongly scented; unfortunately, the fragrance is not altogether pleasant. The petals are green, heavily striped with dark red, and the white lip is spotted with red. It has been important as a base species for producing spring flowering types and is also in the background of some yellow hybrids.

Alone among the cultivated *Cymbidium* species, it has the habit of producing a number of short upright roots, which grow from established roots near the surface of the compost. This feature makes it instantly recognizable from other *Cymbidium* species with otherwise identical habits of growth. 39♦

A widely distributed species found throughout India and in the Philippine Islands. The Indian variety is in general cultivation: the Philippine variety may be offered under the name of *D. heterocarpum*. The type produces stoutish bulbs of medium length and is deciduous in winter, when it needs a definite rest. Water should be discontinued when the leaves turn yellow and drop off naturally. A position of good light is essential during the winter to encourage flowering in the spring. The flowers appear during the early spring months, making it one of the first dendrobiums to flower. The blooms, up to 5cm (2in) across, are creamy-yellow with a buff brown lip covered in short hairs. They are pleasantly fragrant.

During the growing season keep a lookout for red spider mite, which can attack this plant. It is easily propagated from old canes cut into sections, or new plants can be raised from adventitious growths on old canes. Repot after flowering. 40♦

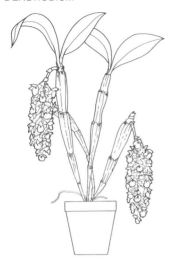 

Dendrobium densiflorum

- ● **Cool: 10°C (50°F)**
- ● **Easy to grow and flower**
- ● **Early summer flowering**
- ● **Evergreen/dry winter rest**

Once plentiful, this delightful species is becoming increasingly difficult to obtain. The flowers, up to 5cm (2in) across, are carried in large pendent trusses from nodes at the top half of the club-shaped bulbs. They develop at great speed during the spring months and last for up to ten days in perfection. Their colour is a brilliant golden yellow, the lip similarly coloured and very striking. The plant likes to be grown in the cool greenhouse with a decided rest in the winter.

The rest period should be commenced as soon as the season's canes have matured and produced new terminal leaf. The plant will flower from the older canes, which may or may not be in leaf. Full light during the autumn and winter is important for regular flowering. Keep the plant dry while in flower to extend flowering.

Not easy to propagate; grow on to a large plant and divide if required. Repot when new growth is seen. This species is evergreen and loses only a few leaves each year. 40♦

Denbrobium Fiftieth State

- ● **Warm: 16-18°C (60-65°F)**
- ● **Moderately easy to grow**
- ● **Summer flowering**
- ● **Evergreen/semi-dry rest**

This fine hybrid illustrates a completely different type of dendrobium, which has been bred from species of Australasian origin. The 6cm (2.4in) flowers of *D. Fiftieth State* are similar in shape to those of *D. phalaenopsis,* although the rich magenta colour of the species appears as overlying veins of soft red in the hybrid. Raised in Hawaii, the plant is warm growing and will succeed in high temperatures and almost full sunlight. It should be watered freely while growing but allowed a complete rest after flowering. The flowers are extremely long-lasting and appear on lengthy sprays from the top of the completed bulb.

Propagation from the old canes is not easy to achieve and the plant should be grown on without division. Do not overpot, or allow undue shrivelling of canes while at rest. Water as required. Repot when new growth has started.

The beautiful flowers may be used for florist's work, and last well when cut and displayed. 40♦

Dendrobium Gatton Sunray

(FCC/RHS)
- **Intermediate: 13°C (55°F)**
- **Moderately easy to grow**
- **Summer flowering**
- **Evergreen/dry winter rest**

A magnificent hybrid, this is the largest of the cultivated dendrobiums, and requires plenty of growing space. It is an extremely robust plant, the canes growing to a height of 2m (6.5ft) or more. The extremely large and showy flowers, which appear in trusses during the early summer, are more than 10cm (4in) across and last in perfection for about ten days. A large plant will produce numerous trusses, each carrying several flowers. This will extend the flowering period, as not all the trusses come into flower at the same time.

The plant succeeds best in an intermediate greenhouse where it can be given good light and a decided rest during the winter months.

This plant is quite rare in cultivation and may take some finding. In view of its large size it should not be attempted where adequate space and light cannot be given. Propagation is very slow. Repot every other year in the spring when the new growth is seen. 41♦

Dendrobium infundibulum

- **Cool: 10°C (50°F)**
- **Easy to grow and flower**
- **Spring flowering**
- **Evergreen/semi-dry rest**

A very fine and distinct species producing large, white flowers, 10cm (4in) across, of a soft papery texture. One to three flowers are produced from each node at the apex of the completed bulb. Well-grown plants produce huge heads of long-lasting flowers, the lip stained with bright yellow in the throat.

D. infundibulum is an evergreen variety and enjoys cool house conditions. In its native India it grows at considerable altitudes. The stems and the sheaths around the young buds are covered in short, protective black hairs.

This plant shrivels easily if kept completely dry for too long during its resting period. Therefore, water sparingly to keep the canes plump at all times. Old leafless canes may appear useless, but should not be removed unless brown and completely shrivelled. Propagation is sometimes possible with older canes. Keep in a small pot and repot after flowering.

The plant will grow well out of doors during the summer months. 42♦

Dendrobium Louisae
- **Warm 16-18°C (60-65°F)**
- **A challenge to grow**
- **Autumn/winter flowering**
- **Evergreen/semi-dry rest**

A very popular plant, this evergreen hybrid is widely grown and is readily available on both sides of the Atlantic. The plant was raised in Indonesia and resulted from the crossing of two showy species native to New Guinea, *D. phalaenopsis* var. *schroederanum* and *D. veratrifolium*, both of which bear long sprays of rose-mauve flowers. *D. Louisae* combines the characteristics of both parents and produces long arching sprays of flowers from the top of the bulbs. The 6cm (2.4in) flowers, which are a rich rose-purple, are extremely long lived and appear during the autumn and winter. The showy flowers can be used in floral arrangements to good effect. The plant can be grown in a warm sun room or greenhouse where it enjoys an abundance of light. Generous growing conditions will produce excellent results.

Propagation is very slow, and not easily achieved from the old canes. The plant should be grown on without division, unless considerably large. Do not overpot. Repot as soon as new growth is seen. 43▸

Dendrobium nobile
- **Cool: 10°C (50°F)**
- **Easy to grow and flower**
- **Spring flowering**
- **Semi-deciduous/dry rest**

Perhaps the most popular of all the cool-growing dendrobiums, this superb plant from India blooms during the spring. The flowers appear in ones and twos along the complete length of the previous year's bulbs, which are fairly tall and stoutish. The flowers, 5cm (2in) across, are rosy purple at the petal tips, shading to white towards the centre of the bloom. The lip carries a rich maroon blotch in the throat.

During the winter rest water should be withheld until the flower buds have clearly started their development in the spring. If watering is started too early embryo flower buds will develop into adventitious growths. Water well all summer, and keep cool. Too high temperatures will restrict flowering.

Propagates easily from leafless canes, or new plants can be raised from adventitious growths. Do not overpot. If the plant becomes top heavy put the pot into a larger weighted container. Repot when new growth appears. 42▸

Dendrobium pierardii
- Intermediate: 13°C (55°F)
- Easy to grow and flower
- Spring flowering
- Deciduous/dry winter rest

A very handsome species from India that produces extremely long, cane-like pseudobulbs that assume a pendent habit unless trained upright in a pot. The plant becomes deciduous during the winter months, when it is important to allow full light to ensure successful flowering the following spring. The 5cm (2in) blooms are produced on the entire length of the previous year's canes and are extremely pretty. They are beautifully coloured a rosy pastel pink, and the rounded lip is creamy yellow, streaked with purple at the base.

This species is at its best when grown into a large plant. Start watering after flowering; adventitious growths are produced if the plant is watered too early in the year. High summer temperatures are necessary to encourage complete growth of the extra long canes. Watch out for red spider mite during the growing season. Regular overhead spraying will help to keep this pest at bay. Do not overpot; does best mounted on bark. Remove old canes only when shrivelled. 43♦

Dendrobium secundum
- Intermediate: 13°C (55°F)
- Easy to grow and flower
- Spring/summer flowering
- Evergreen/semi-dry rest

An extremely pretty and distinctive species with a wide distribution down the Malaysian peninsula and into the Philippine Islands. The unusual flowers are individually very small, clustered tightly together into compact sprays 8-10cm (3.5-4in) long. The rosy pink flowers, with an orange blotch on the lip, appear for an extended period through the spring and summer months. The flower clusters appear from the topmost section of the previous year's canes, which may or may not be in leaf. The same cane can flower for more than one season.

It is a neat and attractive-looking plant with slender well-leafed canes that hold their foliage for several years before shedding a few leaves at a time. It does not propagate readily from old canes; it should be grown on into a large plant and divided only when large enough. Keep in as small a pot as possible. Repot when new growth is seen.

No hybridizing has been done with this species, which may be difficult to find in some areas of the world. 45♦

Dendrobium speciosum

- Intermediate/warm: 13-18°C (55-65°F)
- A challenge to flower
- Spring flowering
- Evergreen/extended dry rest

A most attractive species from Australia, this plant enjoys warmth and humidity during its growing season, with a decided rest during the winter. It is not unusual for this rest period to last for many months. No water should be given while the plant is at rest.

If ripened sufficiently the plant will bloom profusely in the spring, producing a shower of flower spikes bearing many rather small, densely packed flowers, off white in colour with the lip lightly spotted in purple. The flowers have a particularly delightful fragrance.

Not often seen in cultivation, this is a rewarding plant to grow where generous conditions permit. It can attain considerable size and is one of the largest of the genus, although slower growing than most. It does not propagate from old bulbs and should be grown on to a large plant and eventually divided. Repot when new growth is seen.

No hybrids have been produced from this particular species. 44♦

Dendrobium superbum

- Warm: 16-18°C (60-65°F)
- Easy to grow and flower
- Early summer flowering
- Deciduous/dry winter rest

One of the finest dendrobiums from the Philippine Islands, this is a deciduous species that produces extremely long canes. The fragrant flowers appear during the early summer, along the entire length of the previous year's canes; they are 5-6cm (2-2.4in) across, and a rich magenta-purple, the lip a deeper shade. There is also a variety *album*, which produces pure white flowers. Although rarer in cultivation it can sometimes be found. The very long canes make this species ideal for growing upside-down on a wooden raft.

This species will occasionally propagate from old canes, but it is best when grown into a large plant. Be wary of attack from red spider mite during the growing season. When the leaves turn yellow withhold water until flowering starts in the following spring. If grown in a pot, careful staking will be required. Remove old canes only when brown and shrivelled. Repot when the new growth is clearly seen. 44♦

Dendrobium Tangerine 'Tillgates'
(AM/RHS)
- Intermediate: 13°C (55°F)
- Moderately easy to grow
- Spring/summer flowering
- Semi-deciduous/semi-rest

Rather different from the 'traditional' cultivated dendrobium, this outstanding hybrid was raised from a little known but beautiful species, *D. strebloceras,* which comes from western New Guinea. Its name means 'crumpled horn' and refers to the long twisting petals. In the hybrid these petals stand erect, closely resembling the horns of an antelope. The plant is more colourful than its parent species, the 7.5cm (3in) flowers having bright orange petals and mustard yellow sepals and lip. Although the plant is little grown outside the tropics, its unusual and delightful flowers make it a desirable addition to any collection. A subject for the intermediate greenhouse, it would not do well as a houseplant, as it requires full light throughout the year.

The plant is of neat habit, producing elegant canes that are leafed at the top. Flowering is from the top of the canes. It does not propagate readily and should not be hastily divided. 44▶

Dendrobium transparens
- Intermediate: 13°C (55°F)
- Easy to grow and flower
- Spring flowering
- Deciduous/dry winter rest

An extremely pretty and free-flowering species from India that grows well on bark in a pendent position. Its flowers, produced early in the year along the length of the previous season's canes, are 4cm (1.5in) across and pale rosy mauve, the colour heightening towards the tips of the petals; the lip carries two distinctive purple stains. It is a deciduous species which should be well rested before the next spring flowering season. After the leaves have turned yellow do not water until the flowers appear. Where generous summer conditions are provided ample flowering will follow. Watch out for red spider mite during the growing season.

If pot culture is preferred this plant can be beautifully trained into a fan shape. Do not overpot. Adventitious growths are easily produced and can be used for propagation. Otherwise grow into a large plant before dividing. Remove old canes only when brown and shrivelled. Repot after flowering. 45▶

Dendrobium wardianum

- **Cool: 10°C (50°F)**
- **Easy to grow and flower**
- **Winter flowering**
- **Deciduous/dry winter rest**

One of the most handsome of the cool-growing species, this too comes from India. The 5-6cm (2-2.4in) flowers, produced along the length of the previous year's canes, are white, with the petals, sepals and lip tipped with amethyst purple; the lip is also brightly stained with yellow and two maroon blotches at the base. The canes can become tall on a large plant, and it grows well on wooden rafts.

This is another plant that can be affected by red spider mite because of its soft, short-lived foliage. Do not overpot. Water well during the growing season and provide good winter light for successful flowering. Some staking will be necessary if the plant is grown upright in a pot; to prevent it becoming top heavy place the pot in a weighted container. Remove old canes only when brown and shrivelled. It is occasionally possible to propagate the plant from old canes. Repot immediately after flowering, by which time the new growth will be clearly showing. 46♦

Dendrobium williamsonii

- **Cool: 10°C (50°F)**
- **Easy to grow and flower**
- **Spring/summer flowering**
- **Evergreen/semi-dry rest**

This is a stout species whose bulbs do not form very tall canes. Being fairly small in size this is a most adaptable plant that never becomes unmanageable; it grows wider rather than taller. The numerous flowers appear in early summer from the top of the newly completed bulbs and are ivory white, the lip handsomely marked with brick red. They are 4cm (1.5in) across, fragrant and long-lasting.

This species does not propagate easily and is best grown on into a specimen plant, when its full beauty can be appreciated. It will flower with less light than most dendrobiums, and is therefore more suited for indoor culture. Do not overpot. Old canes will often produce a second flowering another year. Do not allow canes to shrivel durings its semi-dry winter rest. Repot immediately new growth is seen.

The plant grows equally well mounted on bark, when it will quickly grow into a large plant, producing several new growths each year. 47♦

Dendrochilum glumaceum
- Cool: 10°C (50°F)
- Easy to grow and flower
- Spring flowering
- Evergreen/semi-dry rest

The *Dendrochilum* genus contains 150 known species, many of which are very attractive. They are frequently given the generic name of *Platyclinis,* but this is now considered to be incorrect. Though dendrochilums are native to a wide area of Southeast Asia, those under cultivation come mainly from the Philippines, where they grow in large clumps on rocks and trees.

Although from a warm climate, these plants do well in the cool house with good protection from full sun. Plenty of moisture at the root is required when the plant is in full growth, but drier conditions should be provided throughout the winter, when it is usually at rest.

The plant develops a small oval pseudobulb that produces a solitary leaf. Thin wiry flower spikes arising from the centre of the new growths grow upright at first, then bend over and hang down, producing two rows of tiny, fragrant, straw-coloured flowers, with perhaps as many as 80 on each spike. This gives rise to the name 'chain orchid'.

Doritis pulcherrima
- Warm: 18°C (65°F)
- Fairly easy to grow
- Varied flowering season
- Evergreen/no rest

A native of Southeast Asia, this species is much prized in modern collections and grows well in warm house conditions suitable for *Phalaenopsis.*

In plant habit and appearance it is much like *Phalaenopsis*, but is inclined to grow taller. It has three to four pairs of stiff grey-green leaves, spotted with dark purple on the upper surface.

The flower spikes are held upright and grow to a height of 60cm (24in) or more, producing ten to 25 flowers which open, a few at a time, on the upper half of the spike. Flowers appear at any season and often more than once in the same year. As individual flowers last for many weeks, a single spike can bloom for four or five months. The flowers vary widely in size (2-4cm; 0.75-1.5in) and colour; the sepals and petals range from pale rose-purple to deep magenta, with parts of the lip often of a deeper hue.

This species has been used extensively in hybridization, particularly with *Phalaenopsis.* 47♦

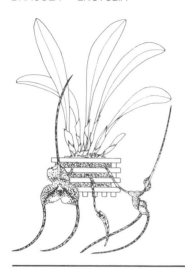

Dracula chimaera
- **Cool: 10°C (50°F)**
- **Moderately easy to grow**
- **Winter/spring flowering**
- **Evergreen/no rest**

Because of the high-altitude conditions of its natural habitat, the cool house with plenty of shade and fresh air during the summer months provides the ideal environment for this plant. As this orchid does not produce pseudobulbs – the thick leaves spring directly from a creeping rhizome – the plant should never be allowed to become dry. Good drainage at the root is also important.

Because this species is inclined to grow in pendent form and down into the compost, it is a good idea to grow the plant in a basket, where the flower spike can come through the sides.

The flowers open one at a time, in succession, on a single spike. Each flower can be from 15-30cm (6-12in) measured vertically, sepals terminating in long tails. They are cream-coloured, lightly or heavily spotted with a deep reddish purple and covered with short purple hairs. The lip is larger in this species, orange-pink in colour, and hinged so that it rocks when the flower moves.

Until recently this plant was included under *Masdevallia*. 46♦

Encyclia citrina
- **Cool: 9°C (48°F)**
- **Moderately easy to grow**
- **Early summer flowering**
- **Semi-deciduous/dry rest**

Often known as *Cattleya citrina,* this Mexican species prefers the well-shaded cool house; it does best growing downwards from a raft or piece of cork bark with very little compost. The pseudobulbs and leaves are greyish-green in colour. Single (or occasionally two), pendent, very fragrant and long-lasting flowers are produced at most times of the year. They are lemon yellow with a deeper yellow centre to the lip, and sometimes a white band on the margin.

Unlike so many orchids, this species prefers to be kept on the dry side all the year round, even while it is growing. Just sufficient water should be given to prevent the pseudobulbs from excessive shrivelling. The plant is totally intolerant of warm conditions. When placed in the genus *Cattleya* and treated as such it was widely considered to deteriorate in cultivation within a few years. Now its cool, dry requirements are more fully appreciated, the plant can easily be grown into a good-sized specimen even by a beginner, provided the above is adhered to.

Encyclia cochleata
- **Cool: 10°C (50°F)**
- **Easy to grow and flower**
- **Varied flowering season**
- **Evergreen/slight rest**

A subject for the cool house, this South American species produces flattened pear-shaped pseudobulbs about 18cm (7in) tall. The flowers resemble the shape of an octopus in water, with their thin green sepals and petals which droop down below the rounded, dark purple, almost black lip.

Several flowers are produced at a time in succession on a flowering spike which, on a large mature plant, can continue flowering for up to two years. Such is the vigour of this species that this in no way impairs its new growth, with the result that two years' flower spikes can be in flower at the same time.

It is one of the few orchids that can be repotted while in bloom. This will be necessary when the new growth has started in the spring.

The old leafless pseudobulbs can be removed for propagation. When potted up singly they will readily develop new growths.

This is an excellent species for beginners; and it can also be grown successfully indoors. 48♦

Encyclia mariae
- **Cool: 9°C (48°F)**
- **Moderately easy to grow**
- **Summer flowering**
- **Semi-deciduous/dry rest**

This species is similar in appearance to *E. citrina* but is grown upright in a pot. One to five flowers are carried on a thin stem, each being about 5cm (2in) wide; the sepals and petals are lime green and the very broad lip, which is often the widest part of the flower, is pure white. *E. mariae* is considered to be one of the loveliest of all the summer-flowering orchids.

The flowers are extremely large for the size of the plant, and last well. The plant should not be heavily watered at any time and is intolerant of soggy conditions. Allow the plant to rest while not in active growth, and keep in a fairly shady aspect. Propagation from the oldest pseudobulbs is slow; it is better to leave them on the plant provided it is healthy. The plant should not be sprayed, as the leaves are susceptible to water marks.

This plant can also be grown on a piece of bark, where it should be allowed to remain undisturbed for a number of years. If too many leafless bulbs build up, these should be removed very carefully without disturbing the plant. 66♦

Encyclia pentotis
- ● **Cool: 10°C (50°F)**
- ● **Shy to flower**
- ● **Early summer flowering**
- ● **Evergreen/semi-rest**

Encyclia vitellina
- ● **Cool: 10°C (50°F)**
- ● **Easy to grow and flower**
- ● **Autumn flowering**
- ● **Evergreen/dry rest**

A beautiful Mexican species that succeeds well in a cool greenhouse or indoors in a position of good light. It has thin cylindrical pseudobulbs which are topped by a pair of slender, dark green leaves. From between the leaves come the flowers, almost stemless. Usually two are produced, back to back with the lip uppermost, resembling alighting butterflies. The lip is cream, streaked with red, and the sepals and petals are creamy white with a slight hint of light green. This very pretty species is beautifully fragrant. The plant can be seen at its best when flowering on a large specimen, when it becomes very free-flowering. Small plants are reluctant to bloom, but a year or two's patience will be amply rewarded when flowering occurs in profusion.

The species grows and propagates easily; several new growths are usually produced each season. Propagation from the old leafless bulbs is possible. The plant may be sprayed in summer and given a semi-dry rest in winter. 65♦

The most colourful of the South American encyclias, this plant likes to be grown under cool house conditions, and will also do well indoors, where it is more tolerant of the drier conditions. The pseudobulbs are oval and carry two blue-green leaves. The flower spike appears at the top of the bulb from between the leaves and grows to 30cm (12in) or more in length on a large plant. At least 12 star-shaped flowers of the most brilliant orange-red are produced on branching stems. The narrow lip, in balance with the rest of the flower, is orange. The blooms are long-lasting, and a colourful sight in the early autumn.

The plant can be grown in a pot or, where greenhouse culture is provided, mounted on a piece of cork bark, where it will make a fine specimen. It will prefer the slightly drier conditions afforded to this type of growing. A dry rest is required for the duration of the winter while the plant is inactive. Overhead spraying is not recommended, as the foliage easily becomes water marked. 66♦

Epidendrum ibaguense

- **Cool: 9°C (48°F)**
- **Easy to grow and flower**
- **Varied flowering season**
- **Evergreen/no rest**

Often known as *E. radicans,* this is a reed-stem species. The stems vary from 60-150cm (2-5ft) in height according to environment and produce rounded leaves and many aerial roots over most of their length. The flowers (2.5cm; 1in) are orange-red or scarlet, the lip flat and very frilled. This is a plant for the cool greenhouse with good light. One successful specimen is known to have flowered continuously for four years.

The epidendrums are one of the largest genera: over 1,000 species are known, coming mainly from Central and South America. So varied are the plants accepted within the genus, in vegetation and flower size and appearance, that some groups have been accorded a genus of their own. Those that remain within the genus are epiphytic.

Epidendrums seem to divide naturally into two categories: those with oval or rounded pseudobulbs, and those that produce reed-like stems. 66♦

Epidendrum stamfordianum

- **Intermediate: 13°C (55°F)**
- **Easy to grow and flower**
- **Early summer flowering**
- **Evergreen/dry rest**

This Central American species produces tall, club-shaped pseudobulbs that carry two or three thick leaves. The branching flower spike comes from the base of the plant, a unique feature among the epidendrums. The flower spike is many flowered; the fragrant blooms are yellow, spotted with red. The plant likes to be grown fairly warm, in a position of good light, and is therefore best suited to an intermediate greenhouse. It should be well watered during the summer growing season and allowed a complete winter's rest. The plant may be grown in a pot or on bark, where it will grow an extensive aerial root system. Propagation is best achieved by division of the main plant when it is large enough.

This large-growing plant is a good example of a bulb-type epidendrum as distinct from the reed type. It is also one of the most attractive epidendrums, although it is not frequently seen in collections. 67♦

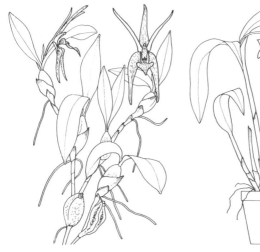

Epigeneium amplum

- **Cool: 10°C (50°F)**
- **Easy to grow and flower**
- **Autumn flowering**
- **Evergreen/semi-dry rest**

An interesting species for the cool house, this plant belongs to a genus of 35 species widely distributed throughout Asia and India. Of these species only two are occasionally seen in cultivation. The genus is considered to be somewhere between the dendrobiums and the bulbophyllums. Oval-shaped pseudobulbs carrying two leaves are produced along an upwardly creeping rhizome. Its root system is surprisingly meagre for an epiphyte; only a few short roots are produced – just sufficient to anchor the plant. A single, richly coloured flower appears on a short stem at the apex of the bulb. The sepals and petals narrow to their tips and are light green in colour overlaid with brown shading. The heart-shaped lip is deep brown, almost to black in some clones.

Because of its creeping habit the plant is not easily accommodated in a pot, but it is ideally suited to life on a piece of bark, where it should be kept moist during the growing season and on the dry side for the rest period during the winter months.

Eria coronaria

- **Cool/intermediate: 10-13°C(50-55°F)**
- **Easy to grow and flower**
- **Spring flowering**
- **Evergreen/semi-rest**

In this species slender stem-like pseudobulbs up to 20cm (8in) in length produce two broad leaves from the apex. Short spikes carry three to five beautifully fragrant flowers 2.5-4cm (1-1.5in) across, which are creamy white in colour with the upper surface of the lip deep purple, marked with yellow.

The species is extremely free-flowering and, although relatively small, its blooms are nevertheless among the largest of the genus. The species is found in India and has long been a favourite in mixed collections.

Like so many orchid species, *Eria coronaria* is at its best when grown into a large specimen plant. Propagation is by division of the main plant. Old bulbs should not be removed until dead, when they will be completely blackened. The compost should be well drained and the plant must never be overwatered; it will fail in overwet conditions.

The plant used to be known under the quite different name of *Trichoma suavis*, but this is no longer in general use.

Above: **Encyclia pentotis**
A lovely summer-flowering species
for the cool house and ideal for the
beginner. The highly fragrant flowers
are long lasting and unusually
attractive. It is a compact grower with
tall, slender bulbs. Also suitable for
growing indoors in good light. 62♦

Above far left: **Encyclia vitellina**
An unusually brightly coloured species suitable for the cool house or indoors. It flowers in the autumn on an upright spray. 62♦

Above left: **Encyclia mariae**
Large showy flowers from a small plant. This species is cool growing and blooms during the summer. Not suitable for beginners. Can also be grown on a piece of bark. 61♦

Above:
Epidendrum stamfordianum
Attractive fragrant flowers on branching spikes from the base. Summer flowering. Thrives in intermediate house conditions. 63♦

Left: **Epidendrum ibaguense**
Can become very tall. A cool-growing, reed-type Epidendrum *that flowers at various times. Will become perpetually blooming.* 63♦

Right: **Eulophia guinensis**
Tall upright spikes are produced in the summer. This beautiful deciduous species will grow well in the warm house. 80♦

Left: **Eria javanica**
An attractive but little known species that likes to grow in the warm. The fragrant blooms appear on sprays during the early spring. 80♦

Below: **Gongora galeata**
This curiously attractive species is cool growing. It flowers freely in the summer on pendent sprays that carry the fragrance of oranges. 82♦

Left: **Gomeza crispa**
A small grower for the cool house. Dainty sprays of flowers appear in the summer. An easy orchid for the beginner. 82♦

Below: **Grammangis ellisii**
A large, robust-growing species for warm-house culture. It blooms in the summer on long arching sprays. Slightly fragrant. 83♦

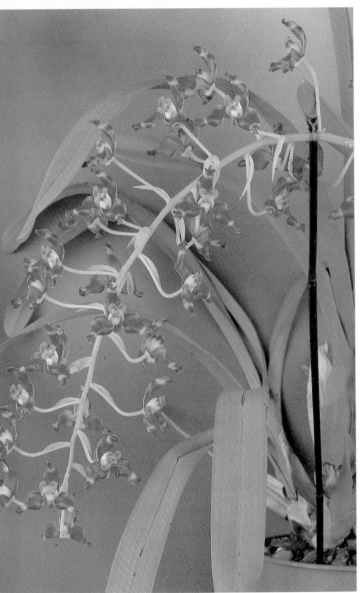

Above: **Laelia cinnabarina**
A neat-growing, intermediate-house species that produces heads of flower in winter/spring. 84♦

Above: **Laelia anceps**
An extremely popular cool-house species ideal for the beginner. Autumn flowering on a tall stem. 84♦

Below: **Huntleya burtii**
A superb species for the inter-mediate house that blooms in the summer. Large single flowers. 83♦

Above: **Laelia gouldiana**
Very popular cool-house species
that blooms in the winter. Several
large flowers are produced atop a tall
stem that emerges from the apex of
the bulb as it completes its growth
during the autumn. Must have good
light to flower successfully. 85♦

Above: **Laeliocattleya Chitchat 'Tangerine'**
This very attractive and unusual hybrid is suitable for the intermediate house. The heads of small brightly coloured flowers appear in the summer. Needs less rest than similar hybrids. 86♦

Top: **Lycaste aromatica**
A deciduous cool-house species that produces its single fragrant blooms in the spring. 86♦

Above: **Lycaste cruenta**
This cool-growing deciduous species has lovely fragrant flowers in the winter and spring. 87♦

Below: **Maclellanara Pagan Lovesong**
A large, robust-growing hybrid for cool or intermediate conditions. 88♦

Above: **Lycaste deppei**
A most attractive plant that produces long-lasting flowers in the winter and spring months. 87♦

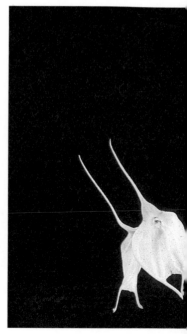

Above: **Lycaste virginalis**
Can be grown in the cool house for winter blooming. Large, single flowers. Deciduous in winter. 88◊

Below: **Masdevallia tovarensis**
A cool-growing species with neat habit. Autumn flowering. The plant blooms again on old stems. 89◊

Left: **Masdevallia coccinea**
A very attractive species for the cool house. The single flowers are carried on a tall, slender stem during the winter and spring. 89▸

Right: **Miltonia Peach Blossom**
This fine hybrid can be grown easily indoors or in an intermediate greenhouse. It flowers at different times of the year. 92▸

Below: **Maxillaria picta**
This species grows in the cool house and blooms during the winter. The single blooms are extremely pretty, fragrant and long lasting. 90▸

Below right: **Maxillaria tenuifolia**
A small-growing, cool-house species that flowers in the summer. It produces short-stemmed, strongly scented flowers. 91▸

Above: **Miltonia clowesii**
*An intermediate species that is
mainly autumn flowering on spikes
up to 60cm (2ft) in height.* 91▶

Above: **Miltonia spectabilis**
*Large single flowers are produced by
this intermediate-house species
during the autumn.* 93▶

Left: **Miltonia roezlii var. alba**
*A rare white form of this species,
now a collector's item. Suitable for
the intermediate greenhouse.* 92♦

Above: **Odontioda Dalmar
'Lyoth Bachus'**
*This cool-house hybrid flowers at
various times of the year.* 93♦

Above:
Odontoglossum cervantesii
This is a small and delightful cool-growing species which blooms over a long period during the winter and spring. The flowers are extremely large for the size of the plant; they are produced on short sprays. 95♦

Eria javanica
- **Warm: 18°C (65°F)**
- **Easy to grow and flower**
- **Winter/spring flowering**
- **Evergreen/semi-rest**

This is a particularly showy species. The pseudobulbs are about 7.5cm (3in) in height, and produce two upright leaves, 30-60cm (1-2ft) in length. An erect flower spike develops to a height of 60cm (2ft) from the top of the pseudobulb, and many well-spaced flowers are produced. These are about 4cm (1.5in) across and creamy green in colour.

Although there are some 500 species of *Eria,* most coming from India or Malaysia, not many are found in collections today. This is surprising as some are very showy and generally they are not difficult to cultivate.

A few species will grow in cool conditions but most do well in the intermediate or warm section of the greenhouse. Some require shade, but others enjoy full light. Most require a period of rest at the completion of their growing season and will flower more freely if this can be given in cooler conditions than those in which the plant has been grown. The flowers of some erias are very short lived; this species is longer lasting than most. 68◆

Eulophia guinensis
- **Warm: 18°C (65°F)**
- **Fairly easy to grow**
- **Summer flowering**
- **Deciduous/dry rest**

Most of the 200 known species of *Eulophia* come from tropical and sub-tropical Africa, and almost all are terrestrial. The genus can be divided roughly into two groups according to vegetation and flower form.

In the first, the plants have a broad, pear-shaped pseudobulb that produces fairly long deciduous leaves that fall when the growing period is completed. The sepals and petals of the flowers are small in comparison with the lip, which is the main attraction.

This species belongs to the first group and is probably the most familiar. After a cool, dry rest throughout the winter the plant should be brought into the warm house and encouraged into growth by light and watering. When growth is still in progress, the flower spike appears and grows to a height of 60-90cm (2-3ft), producing six to 15 flowers. The lip is 2.5-4cm (1-1.5in) in diameter, spade-shaped and rose-pink with darker veins. The sepals and petals are recurving, short and narrow, dullish-purple in colour with green veins.

Gomeza crispa

- **Cool: 10°C (50°F)**
- **Easy to grow and flower**
- **Summer/autumn flowering**
- **Evergreen/no rest**

Although there are about ten species of this epiphytic orchid available to growers, only one, *Gomeza crispa,* from Brazil is grown.

It is a plant for the cool house, requiring some protection from full light during the summer months. Free drainage for the root system is of great importance and for this reason it is a good subject to grow on a raft or piece of cork bark. If grown in a pot, a coarse material, such as fir bark, should be used. As the plant grows upwards, away from the pot, the roots should be allowed to grow outside, where they should gain sufficient nourishment from the atmosphere. Spraying during the summer is helpful.

The plant produces pseudobulbs and leaves similar to those of odontoglossums, only paler in colour. The flowers are carried on arching sprays, up to 23cm (9in) long, and there are often two sprays to a pseudobulb. The sweetly scented, lime-green flowers, about 1.25cm (0.5in) across, are densely clustered on the spike and appear during the summer and autumn. 69♦

Gongora galeata

- **Cool/intermediate: 10-13°C (50-55°F)**
- **Easy to grow and flower**
- **Summer flowering**
- **Evergreen/semi-rest**

These plants are to be found throughout South America from Mexico to Brazil, where they grow as epiphytes. About 12 species are known. Of these, a very few are occasionally found in cultivation. *Gongora galeata* is both interesting and showy as well as being highly fragrant. The fragrance is of oranges.

The plant has a neat habit with oval-shaped, ribbed pseudobulbs, each carrying two slender leaves and a fine rooting system. The flower spikes are extremely thin and can pass unnoticed in their early stage of development or be mistaken for a new root. They develop downwards, so the plant should always be placed in an open basket to allow the spikes freedom to grow. They extend to about 15cm (6in) below the plant and produce up to six or eight flowers. The curiously shaped flowers are about 5cm (2in) long and are usually tawny yellow to buff orange in colour.

The plant should be well watered during its summer growing season, and lightly fed. A position of good light will suit it at all times, especially during the winter. 68♦

Grammangis ellisii
- **Warm: 18°C (65°F)**
- **Moderately easy to grow**
- **Summer flowering**
- **Evergreen/semi-rest**

Huntleya burtii
- **Intermediate: 13°C (55°F)**
- **Can be difficult to grow**
- **Summer flowering**
- **Evergreen/no rest**

This species is a member of a small genus of remarkably handsome epiphytic orchids of which five species are known. It is a large robust plant that requires plenty of room in which to grow. The pseudobulbs are tall, spindle-shaped and four-sided, which is an unusual feature. Several long, leathery leaves are set towards the top half of the bulb. The flower spikes emerge from the half-completed new growth during the summer. These are naturally arching and many flowered. The slightly fragrant flowers are 9cm (3.5in) across and similar in shape to a *Lycaste* flower. The prominent sepals are basically yellow, this colour partially obscured by dense, reddish brown bars. The petals and lip are smaller.

The plant is suitable for a warm greenhouse and while growing should be watered and fed liberally. During the winter less water but extra light should be given. The plants do not like disturbance and should only be repotted when absolutely necessary. The plant is a native of Madagascar. 69♦

This South American plant grows without pseudobulbs. The leaves, about 30cm (12in) in length, develop from a central stem in the form of a fan. Single flowers 6.5-7.5cm (2.5-3in) across, are produced on a 15cm (6in) stem. The sepals and petals are approximately equal in size and uniform in marking; at the base they are greenish-white, changing through yellow to a reddish-brown marked with yellow. The lower half of the lip is reddish-brown, graduating to white in the upper part. These flowers are thick and waxy in texture and last well.

Huntleya burtii has a reputation for being rather difficult to maintain in good condition, but failure is often due to one of two reasons. The first is that many growers have a tendency to keep the plant in too warm and humid an environment, causing it to rot; the second is that the new growths which develop part way up the stem are often mistakenly removed and repotted. It is far better to allow the plant to grow into a clump, and to let the roots from new growths develop as aerial roots. 70♦

Laelia anceps
- ● **Cool: 10°C (50°F)**
- ● **Easy to grow and flower**
- ● **Autumn flowering**
- ● **Evergreen/dry winter rest**

Some 75 species of *Laelia* have been recorded, almost all from Mexico and the northern parts of South America. Though in appearance both plant and flower are similar to the cattleyas, with which many intergeneric hybrids have been made, it is a delightful genus in its own right, and is favoured by many growers. As with cattleyas, its flower spikes are produced from the apex of the pseudobulbs. The flower spike grows erect to 60cm (2ft) or more and produces two to five flowers, each about 10cm (4in) across. They are pale or deep rose-pink in colour, the lip being a darker hue than the other segments.

This is an excellent species for the beginner. It can be grown easily in a cool greenhouse or indoors, where it enjoys light conditions. If preferred, it can be grown on a block of wood or cork bark, when an extensive aerial root system will develop.

Propagation is a simple matter of separating the back bulbs and potting them up singly, when they will develop new growths. 70♦

Laelia cinnabarina
- ● **Intermediate: 13°C (55°F)**
- ● **Moderately easy to grow**
- ● **Winter/spring flowering**
- ● **Evergreen/semi-dry rest**

This plant comes from Brazil and belongs to a group of brilliantly coloured species that are smaller in the size of their plants and flowers than the majority of laelias. This species has thin pseudobulbs, which are darker in colour than most, as is the leaf. Five to 12 star-shaped, orange-red flowers, each about 5cm (2in) across, are produced on a 23cm (9in) spike during the winter and spring. Due to importing restrictions this species is not now often seen in cultivation.

It likes intermediate conditions and is intolerant of cold and damp. The slender pseudobulbs will quickly shrivel if the plant is allowed to remain in a dry state for any length of time. It should be only semi-rested in winter, with sufficient water to ensure that the bulbs remain plump. The plant should be kept in as small a pot as possible and grown on into a good-sized plant. Propagation is by division when the plant is large enough.

This species has been used to some extent in interbreeding to increase colour in the hybrids. 70♦

Laelia gouldiana
- **Cool/intermediate: 10-13°C (50-55°F)**
- **Easy to grow and flower**
- **Winter flowering**
- **Evergreen/dry winter rest**

One of the most popular of the epiphytic Mexican laelias. The club-shaped pseudobulbs are topped with one or — more often — two stiff, dark green leaves that are pointed at their tips. The flower spike appears from the apex of the partially completed bulb during the autumn and grows to 45cm (18in) in height carrying three to five brightly coloured 7.5cm (3in), cattleya-like flowers. Their colouring is a rich rose-purple, the lip similarly coloured. They last for several weeks during the early half of the winter.

This species is suitable for the warmest end of the cool greenhouse, or it will be equally at home in the intermediate section in a position of good light. Light is very important for successful flowering and for this reason it does not always flower well as a house plant. Plants are at their best when grown on into large specimens; continued division can cause them to miss a flowering season. The spring growth is often slow to start and it may be summer before they really get going. 71♦

Laelia purpurata
- **Intermediate: 13°C (55°F)**
- **Easy to grow and flower**
- **Winter flowering**
- **Evergreen/dry winter rest**

This orchid is the national flower of Brazil and deserves the honour. Growing to a height of 45-60cm (1.5-2ft) including the leaf, the plant produces a short spike of two to six flowers, each 13-18cm (5-7in) in diameter. Very variable in colour, the narrow sepals and petals range from white to pale purple, with a frilled deep purple lip.

Moderate light is required and a well-drained compost is important; no laelia does well if there is an excess of water at the root. The plant requires a definite period of rest, when little or no water should be given.

This species has always been extremely popular with collectors but it is now becoming increasingly difficult to obtain. Many commercial nurseries are now raising it from seed using selected clones. Therefore, it should not die out in cultivation in the foreseeable future.

In the past this species has contributed to the production of many intergeneric hybrids with cattleyas and allied genera.

Laeliocattleya Chitchat 'Tangerine'
● **Intermediate: 13°C (55°F)**
● **Moderately easy to grow**
● **Summer flowering**
● **Evergreen/some rest**

A summer-flowering hybrid bred from a cross between *C. aurantiaca* and *Laelia* Coronet. The plant, which has clusters of delicate yellow-orange flowers 5cm (2in) across, has slender pseudobulbs and should be grown in the intermediate section of the greenhouse.

This hybrid illustrates the diversity that can be found among the bigeneric cattleya hybrids. Here we see the less flamboyant flower with simpler lines, but with the superb colouring unique to the type. Also, having one species parent, the plant shows close resemblance to that species.

This plant grows in the same conditions as other cattleya intergeneric hybrids, but will usually have a shorter resting period. The pseudobulbs are more slender and will therefore shrivel more easily if water is withheld for long periods. Light overhead spraying is an advantage during the summer.

Repotting should be carried out in the spring unless the plant is in bud, in which case it should be repotted in the autumn. 72♦

Lycaste aromatica
● **Cool/intermediate: 10-13°C (50-55°F)**
● **Easy to grow and flower**
● **Winter/spring flowering**
● **Deciduous/dry winter rest**

As the name suggests, this species is heavily scented. The bright yellow flowers, 5cm (2in) across, often appear at the same time as the new growth, and are carried singly on a stem about 15cm (6in) long. There may be as many as ten flowers to each pseudobulb.

The plant needs moisture and warmth when in full growth, but take care not to get water on the large, broad leaves, as they tend to develop brown spots if this occurs. Cooler and drier conditions are essential when the plant is at rest and in flower.

Propagation is by removal of the older pseudobulbs, which should not remain on the plant for too many years. It is better to restrict the size of the plant to five or six bulbs, provided they remain about the same size; should the bulbs become smaller, remove all but three or four.

Between 30 and 40 *Lycaste* species are known, including both terrestrial and epiphytic plants, most of which come from Central America. Many are also deciduous, losing their leaves during the winter. 73♦

Lycaste cruenta

- **Cool/intermediate:
  10-13°C (50-55°F)**
- **Easy to grow and flower**
- **Winter/spring flowering**
- **Deciduous/dry winter rest**

A beautiful and fragrant species with the typical *Lycaste* foliage and habit of flowering. The flowers are among the largest of the cultivated species and are beautifully coloured. The sepals are yellow-green, the smaller petals and lip deep golden yellow. There is a deep red stain just visible in the throat.

In all species of *Lycaste* the sepals open wide and are longer than the petals, which are inclined to remain partly closed.

Like all lycastes, the plant enjoys higher summer temperatures while in active growth, followed by a cooler resting period. It should be given as much light as possible without burning the foliage. The leaves, which can be extremely large and spreading when mature, quickly turn yellow in the late autumn and are discarded naturally by the plant.

Annual repotting is beneficial to this species, which can quickly outgrow its pot with one season's growth. The plant is best suited to greenhouse culture, where it is a most rewarding plant to grow. 73♦

Lycaste deppei

- **Cool/intermediate:
  10-13°C (50-55°F)**
- **Easy to grow and flower**
- **Winter/spring flowering**
- **Deciduous/dry winter rest**

One of the most attractive of the lycastes, this plant produces fewer but larger, longer lasting flowers than *L. aromatica* – up to 11.5cm (4.5in) in diameter. The sepals are mid-green in colour spotted with reddish-brown, and the smaller petals are pure white. The lip is yellow in colour and also spotted with reddish-brown.

The plant has a fast growing season, when it should be given slightly higher temperatures combined with ample watering and feed. When repotting, a little old dried cow manure can be included in the compost. Repotting is best done annually; because of the extended dry rest period fresh compost is essential. The leaves, which can grow quite large, should be kept dry at all times; they are susceptible to water marks, which will show as ugly black or brown patches. While in growth, the plants will take up rather more room in the greenhouse. Because they require warmer growing conditions and cooler winter quarters with high light, they are not so easy to grow indoors. 74♦

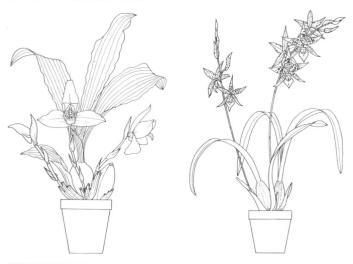

Lycaste virginalis
- Cool/intermediate:
  10-13°C (50-55°F)
- Easy to grow and flower
- Winter/spring flowering
- Deciduous/dry winter rest

The flowers of *L. virginalis,* also known as *L. skinneri,* are even larger – up to 15cm (6in) across. Many colour forms are known and all are beautiful. The colour varies from all-white (which is rare) through pale to deep pink, and the lip is often spotted with crimson.

This is the most popular species of the genus and is ideal for beginners to orchid growing. It is easier to grow indoors than the other lycastes. It does not like to be overwet at any time and must be kept completely dry during the winter. The flowers of this lovely orchid bruise easily and quickly become spotted if the humidity is high. This plant usually retains its season's growth throughout the winter, resting in an evergreen state to shed its foliage immediately the new growth starts in the spring. Propagation is by removal of the back pseudobulbs. The plant is at its best when kept to about six bulbs.

There are excellent hybrids from this species, especially with the intergeneric angulocastes. 75♦

Maclellanara Pagan Lovesong
- Cool/intermediate:
  10-13°C (50-55°F)
- Easy to grow and flower
- Varied flowering season
- Evergreen/no rest

This is one of the latest and most impressive of the man-made intergeneric hybrids. It was raised in the USA from *Odontocidium* Tiger Butter x *Brassia verrucosa* and therefore contains three genera in its make-up – *Odontoglossum, Oncidium* and *Brassia.* The plant resembles a large *Odontoglossum* and is a vigorous and robust grower tolerant of both cool and intermediate conditions. It can be grown in almost any climate. The flower spikes can be over 90cm (3ft) tall with up to 12 large, exciting 10cm (4in) flowers that exhibit much influence from the *Brassia.* The sepals and petals are of equal size, yellow-green with large dark brown occasional spots. The handsome lip is white and spotted in a similar way.

Maclellanaras are all year round growers and should be freely watered and fed throughout the year. They should receive similar light to odontoglossums. The plants are becoming extremely popular although they are still very limited in supply in some countries.74♦

Masdevallia coccinea
- Cool: 10°C (50°F)
- Moderately easy to grow
- Winter/spring flowering
- Evergreen/no rest

Masdevallia tovarensis
- Cool: 10°C (50°F)
- Moderately easy to grow
- Autumn flowering
- Evergreen/no rest

This is one of the most fascinating orchid genera, as remarkable for the uniformity of its vegetation as for the diversity of form and colour of its flowers. Three hundred species are recorded, growing mainly in the higher-altitude areas of Mexico, Brazil and Colombia. The structure of the flowers is in contrast to that of many orchids, as the sepals are very large in comparison with the other segments of the flower.

This species produces leaves 30cm (12in) in length, and the flower spikes are often much taller. These bear a single flower of 7.5-10cm (3-4in), with sepals that taper sharply towards the tips. The colour varies from lilac to deep crimson.

Because of the high-altitude conditions of its natural habitat, the cool house with plenty of shade and fresh air during the summer months provides the ideal environment. Masdevallias do not produce pseudobulbs – the thick leaves spring directly from a creeping rhizome – so the plants should never be allowed to become dry. 76♦

A beautiful species from Colombia that produces the typical neat growth of the genus. The leaves are glossy, dark green and grow from the base of the plant from a connecting rhizome. The flowering stems come from the base of the leaves and carry two to four flowers clear of the foliage. When the flowers have died, the stem remains green and blooms again the following year, an unusual feature for an orchid. The attractive flowers are a soft powdery white and are largely composed of the three sepals, which are elongated and end with a short tail.

Odontoglossum-type culture suits these orchids well. They should be grown in cool, airy conditions and kept just moist at all times. The plants will quickly deteriorate if allowed to get too wet or too cold at any time. A well-drained compost and regular repotting are essential. Several new growths will be produced each growing season, enabling a large plant to be built up in a comparatively short time. Propagation is by division when the plant is large enough. 75♦

Maxillaria picta
- Cool: 10°C (50°F)
- Easy to grow and flower
- Winter flowering
- Evergreen/dry winter rest

Maxillaria porphyrostele
- Cool/intermediate: 10-13°C (50-55°F)
- Easy to grow and flower
- Winter/spring flowering
- Evergreen/semi-rest

This is one of the prettiest and most popular of the genus. The plant has roundish pseudobulbs topped by two long, narrow leaves. The 5cm (2in) flowers, produced prolifically on single stems, are yellow on the inside of the sepals and petals. On the outside are reddish-brown bars that show through to the inside. The lip is creamy white and slightly spotted in red. This lovely species flowers in profusion during the middle of the winter and has a pleasant, strong fragrance.

During the summer the plant should be kept moist and lightly fed, with a decided rest in good light after the season's growth is completed. The flowering stems appear at the same time as the new growths, the stems being rounded and fatter. Several new growths can be produced in a season, resulting in a good-sized plant within a few years. Propagation is by division of the plant when large enough. This pretty orchid can be grown in a cool greenhouse or indoors.76♦

This species is very easy to accommodate as it will grow into a specimen plant without needing too much space. It is best grown in a wire or wooden basket, because it grows prolifically and in time will not only cover the top of its container but also grow over the sides.

Plants produce clusters of pseudobulbs with broad leaves that develop from a horizontal rhizome. Each leading pseudobulb can produce a number of short flower spikes, which carry a yellow flower of 4cm (1.5in) diameter. The tips of both sepals and petals are incurving. The flowers are long-lasting, and appear from winter to spring.

About 300 species of this very diverse genus are known. They are widely scattered throughout tropical America and almost all are epiphytic. This genus is well-known to many growers, not only for its interesting flowers, but also for the variety of their scent.

Grow in good light and overhead spray during the summer.

Maxillaria tenuifolia
- ● Cool: 10°C (50°F)
- ● Easy to grow and flower
- ● Summer flowering
- ● Evergreen/semi-dry rest

Miltonia clowesii
- ● Intermediate: 13°C (55°F)
- ● Fairly easy to grow
- ● Autumn/varied flowering
- ● Evergreen/no rest

In this species a creeping rhizome, which grows almost vertically, produces small oval pseudobulbs at 2.5-5cm (1-2in) intervals. The flowers, 2.5cm (1in) across, are dark or bright red speckled with yellow. The plant has a very strong scent similar to that of coconut.

Because of its creeping habit it will quickly grow out of its pot and it is therefore more easily accommodated on a slab of wood. Grown vertically in this way, the plant quickly makes itself at home. It makes new roots sparingly and usually from the older bulbs around its base. The flowers, though not numerous, cluster around the bulbs on extremely short stems. Their bright colouring makes them eye-catching.

This is a plant that thrives in light conditions and dislikes too much moisture around its base. A well-drained compost is important if the plant is grown in a pot. During the summer it can be kept just moist by overhead spraying.77♦

This is a Brazilian plant, with pseudobulbs, whose leaves reach a height of about 50cm (20in). The flower spike, which may be up to 60cm (2ft) in length, grows from the base of the pseudobulb and bears six to ten flowers, each about 6.5cm (2.5in) across. The sepals and petals are of equal size, reddish-brown and barred with yellow. The lip, in direct contrast, is white with a pinky-mauve blotch on its upper part.

Twenty species of this deservedly popular genus have been recorded. The majority are very sweet-scented and flower throughout the year, often more than once. They divide roughly into two natural groups. In the first group are plants from Brazil, which produce yellowish-green foliage and flattened pseudobulbs, well spaced on a creeping rhizome. These orchids require intermediate conditions and more light than plants in the second group, which grow in the higher regions of Colombia.

Propagation is by division when the plant is large enough. 78♦

Miltonia Peach Blossom
- Intermediate: 13°C (55°F)
- Moderately easy to grow
- Varied flowering season
- Evergreen/no rest

Miltonia roezlii
- Intermediate: 13°C (55°F)
- Moderately easy to grow
- Autumn flowering
- Evergreen/no rest

This is a typical *Miltonia* hybrid produced from the soft-leaved Colombian species commonly known as the 'pansy orchids'. These hybrids come in a wide variety of colours — white, yellow, pink and red. Peach Blossom is one of the most popular varieties with large, plum red flowers, the colour shading to white towards the edges of the flower.

This orchid and other similar hybrids should be grown in an intermediate greenhouse or a warm room. Their dislike of cold, damp conditions makes them ideally suited to the drier atmosphere in the home. Watering should be on a continuous basis; never allow the plants to dry out completely. The foliage should not be sprayed and feeding should be applied to the pot when watering. One weak feed every three weeks during the spring and summer should be sufficient.

Repotting should be done when the new growth is showing, which may be spring or autumn. 77♦

This extremely pretty plant is one of the soft-leaved Colombian species. It produces the typical neat oval pseudobulbs of the type and these are partially covered by soft, silver-green leaves. The flower spike appears from inside the first or second leaf on the newly completed bulb and carries two to four white flowers. The two lateral petals are painted purple at their bases and the lip has a yellow blotch that spreads out from the centre, or 'mask'. Although this plant is quite rare, supplies should be available from nursery-raised stock.

Although this species likes fairly warm conditions, it should not be allowed to suffer from too high temperatures. The intermediate section of the cool house will suit it. A beginner would find the many superb hybrids that have been raised from this species tolerant and easy to grow.

There is also a rare *alba* variety, which lacks the purple colouring at the base of the petals. 78♦

Miltonia spectabilis
- **Intermediate: 13°C (55°F)**
- **Fairly easy to grow**
- **Autumn/varied flowering**
- **Evergreen/no rest**

Another Brazilian species, this orchid resembles *M. clowesii,* but the flower spike grows to no more than 25cm (10in) in length and bears fewer, slightly larger, flowers which are white or pinky-white, with a broad, flat, purple lip.

Miltonia spectabilis var. *moreliana* is a distinct variety of this plant, and is more often seen today than the pure species. Its flower is an overall deep purple in colour with a lighter hue on the lip.

The plant has a rather untidy habit of growth and will quickly spread over the edge of its pot. It can make a grand specimen when attached to a flat piece of wood and allowed to grow on unhindered. It likes to be grown in good light and it is natural for the whole plant to take on a yellowish appearance. Given the right conditions, this is a robust grower and it passes on many of its good qualities when used for hybridization.

Propagation can be carried out by the removal of back bulbs. 78♦

Odontioda Dalmar 'Lyoth Bachus'
(FCC/RHS)
- **Cool: 10°C (50°F)**
- **Easy to grow and flower**
- **Varied flowering season**
- **Evergreen/no rest**

When the highly coloured odontiodas are crossed with large well-formed odontoglossum hybrids the results are a culmination of two lines of breeding, superbly illustrated by this most magnificent of plants. This hybrid has beautiful deep red flowers edged with pale mauve and 10cm (4in) across. The odontioda parent is Margia, which has been influenced by the *Cochlioda noezliana* in its background, whereas the odontoglossum parent, Mandalum, has *O. crispum* in its immediate ancestry.

This hybrid requires cool growing conditions in a position of good light. These plants do not divide or propagate very easily and should be grown on into as large a specimen as possible. Leafless pseudobulbs should not be allowed to outnumber those in leaf and are always better removed when this stage is reached. Regular repotting is essential to ensure the compost remains fresh.

Further, excellent hybrids have been produced from this one. 79♦

93

Odontocidium Tigersun 'Nutmeg'
- Cool/intermediate: 10-13°C (50-55°F)
- Easy to grow and flower
- Varied flowering season
- Evergreen/no rest

The introduction of *Oncidium* species into the breeding of odontoglossum hybrids has increased in popularity over the last few years and many hybrids are becoming available. Apart from giving different types of flowers and colours, most of the odontocidiums will stand more extreme conditions than the pure odontoglossums – which is of great importance to growers in warmer climates or where a mixed collection is cultivated. *Odontocidium* Tigersun is a cross between *Oncidium tigrinum* (a popular scented species from Mexico) and *Odontoglossum* Sunmar, and produces excellent bright yellow flowers, 9cm (3.5in) across, of good substance.

In common with other intergeneric odontoglossums, this hybrid does not have a definite resting period. It should be watered throughout the year, although less so during the winter. The only time this plant is not growing is while it is in flower, which can be six or eight weeks. 97♦

Odontoglossum bictoniense
- Cool: 10°C (50°F)
- Easy to grow and flower
- Summer flowering
- Evergreen/semi-rest

This is one of the easiest and most popular species, and an ideal plant for beginners. Native to Guatemala, it is a very vigorous grower and will quickly grow into a specimen plant. Erect flower spikes appear at the end of the summer, growing quickly in warm weather to reach heights up to 122cm (48in) and bearing 20 long-lasting flowers on each spike. The flowers open in succession so that there are usually eight or nine out at once over a period of several weeks. The flowers are about 3-4cm (1.25-1.5in) across, yellowy green with brown spots and a striking white or pink lip.

O. bictoniense, which can be grown successfully as a houseplant, requires cool conditions with medium shade and does not need resting in winter, though water should be reduced when flowering has finished, until new growth appears in the spring.

This species is very variable. The plant is easily propagated from the leafless pseudobulbs. 97♦

Odontoglossum cervantesii

- ● **Cool: 10°C (50°F)**
- ● **Easy to grow and flower**
- ● **Winter/spring flowering**
- ● **Evergreen/slight rest**

A delightful dwarf species from Mexico. The total height of pot, bulbs and leaves is only about 15cm (6in) and makes this an ideal subject for growers with limited space.

The flowers are produced on semi-pendent spikes, in winter and early spring, from the new growth as it starts to form a pseudobulb. In comparison to the size of the plant, the flowers are large – about 4 – 5cm (1.5 – 2in) across, beautifully white, almost round and marked with a distinctive band of chestnut rings towards the middle of the sepals and petals.

Being a species with fine roots it does not like to dry out during the growing season and thrives in a fine but free-draining compost. During the winter months water should be reduced and a small amount of shrivelling of the bulb is normal at this time. Give medium shade during the summer.

This species is at its best when allowed to grow on into a large plant. It can also be grown on bark. 80♦

Odontoglossum crispum

- ● **Cool: 10°C (50°F)**
- ● **Moderately easy to grow**
- ● **Varied flowering season**
- ● **Evergreen/slight rest**

Coming from high up in the Andes, this plant needs medium to heavy shade and cool, moist, humid conditions. The large flowers, up to 10cm (4in) across, vary considerably in presence or absence of marking. Flower spikes develop from the side of the new bulb as it is forming and, as the seasons in its native environment are not clearly defined and growth can start at any time, the flowers may open at virtually any time of year, though spring and autumn are probably the most common.

Selective breeding of varieties has been continuing for many years and this has ensured that *Odontoglossum crispum* will still be available to enthusiasts without calling on the dwindling wild stocks; moreover, these cultivated plants are of higher quality. As an ancestor, *Odontoglossum crispum* has probably contributed more towards improving the flower size and shape of *Odontoglossum* and *Odontioda* hybrids than any other species. 97♦

Odontoglossum Gold Cup 'Lemon Drop'
- Cool: 10°C (50°F)
- Fairly easy to grow
- Autumn flowering
- Evergreen/no rest

This cross between *Odontoglossum* Chamois Snowcrest and *O. Crowbrough Sunrise* is a good example of yellow odontoglossum breeding. The flowers are 6cm (2.4in) across, and a bright canary yellow with a few golden brown markings on the lip. The plant, which is proving to be a good parent in its turn, requires cool conditions with plenty of shade during the summer.

Being a pure-bred *Odontoglossum* this plant is less tolerant of varying conditions, and thus more attention must be paid to its cultural requirements. A cool, light and airy atmosphere is important at all times, conditions which are more easily obtained with the aid of a greenhouse. The flowers, which can last for a good six to eight weeks, are ideal for all florist's work, and will last for the same length of time if cut and placed in water.

An open, well-draining compost is very important. The plant should be kept watered throughout the year and never allowed to become completely dry. 99♦

Odontoglossum grande
- Cool: 10°C (50°F)
- Easy to grow and flower
- Autumn flowering
- Evergreen/dry winter rest

Known widely as the 'clown orchid' due to the clown-like figure represented by the column in the centre of the flower, this is certainly one of the most widely grown in this genus, and popular as a houseplant. The flowers are very large, up to 15cm (6in) across, yellow with bright chestnut-brown markings.

It has hard dark leaves and very tough pseudobulbs, and needs a decided rest during the winter months. During the growing season it needs plenty of moisture at the roots but excessive atmospheric moisture can result in unsightly black spotting on the foliage. As the new growth starts to make a pseudobulb towards the end of the summer the flower spike develops, and the flowers usually open in autumn. Once flowering is finished and the pseudobulbs have fully matured, watering should be withheld until spring, when the new growth appears. The plants need light shade and should be grown in a medium-grade bark compost. They should receive full light in winter. 98♦

Above: **Odontoglossum crispum**
*An easy cool-house species that
flowers at various times of the year.
Long-lasting sprays.* 95♦

Below: **Odontocidium Tigersun
'Nutmeg'**
*An easy-to-grow hybrid for a cool
greenhouse or indoor culture.* 94♦

Below:
Odontoglossum bictoniense
*Tall, upright spikes are produced by
this cool-growing, late summer-
flowering species. Easy.* 94♦

Left: **Odontoglossum rossii**
A delightful miniature species for the cool greenhouse. It produces lovely long-lasting flowers in winter. 113♦

Below left:
Odontoglossum grande
This very popular species is cool growing. The very large showy flowers appear during the autumn months. Easy to grow. 96♦

Right:
Odontoglossum pulchellum
This attractive cool-house species is spring flowering. Sprays of small, waxy, fragrant blooms. 113♦

Below: **Odontoglossum Gold Cup 'Lemon Drop'**
This cool-growing hybrid produces sprays of large flowers mainly during the autumn months. 96♦

Above: **Oncidium ornithorynchum**
*A pretty miniature species for the
cool house. It produces fragrant
sprays of flowers in the autumn.* 115♦

Below: **Paphiopedilum callosum**
*This 'slipper orchid' blooms in the
spring and summer. Ideal for
intermediate conditions.* 117♦

Above: **Oncidium papilio**
The famous 'butterfly orchid', it
grows in the warm house and flowers
at various times. The flowers appear
in succession one at a time from the
top of a tall slender stem. This
species is not suitable for a
beginner; it requires specialist
treatment to be kept in good health.
Flowers up to 13cm (5in) across. 116♦

Above:
Paphiopedilum hirsutissimum
*This species has neat foliage and a
single, large, very long-lasting
flower. It is cool growing and blooms
in the early summer months.* 119♦

Above right:
Paphiopedilum insigne
*This popular species is easy to grow
in a cool greenhouse or indoors. One
or two long-lasting flowers per stem
from autumn to spring.* 120♦

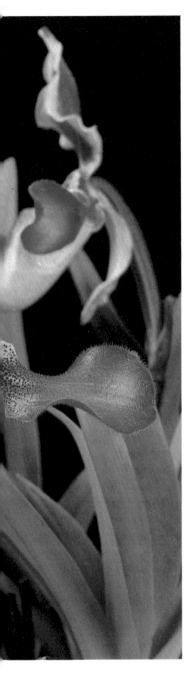

Right:
Paphiopedilum rothschildianum
*An exciting but rare species for the
intermediate greenhouse. Blooms
during the summer and autumn on
upright sprays.* 122♦

Left: **Paphiopedilum delenatii**
This attractive summer-flowering species belongs in the intermediate to warm greenhouse. It is compact and fragrant. 118♦

Right: **Paphiopedilum Honey Gorse 'Sunshine'**
For the intermediate house, this winter-flowering hybrid produces a single, large flower per stem. 119♦

Below: **Paphiopedilum Maudiae**
This graceful flower is carried on a slender stem at various times of the year. Will grow well in intermediate house conditions. 120♦

Above: **Paphiopedilum parishii**
Not all paphiopedilums produce single flowers, as can be seen in this species with its long sprays of elegant flowers. The plant is an easy *orchid to grow in the intermediate house. It blooms over a long period during the winter months of the year. It is a fairly large-growing plant; the stem may be 60cm (2ft) high.* 121♦

Left: **Paphiopedilum Miller's Daughter 'Snow Maiden'**
A lovely white-flowered variety for the intermediate house. One or two exquisite flowers are produced during the winter months. A beautiful and vigorous plant. 121♦

Below: **Paphiopedilum Royale 'Downland'**
This is an excellent red-flowered variety for the intermediate house. The single blooms are very long lasting during the winter months of the year. 122♦

Above: **Paphiopedilum venustum**
*An attractive compact-growing
species for the intermediate house.
Flowers during the spring. Will thrive
in shady and airy conditions.* 123♦

Below:
Phalaenopsis Barbara Moler
*This warm-house hybrid produces
sprays of flowers in the spring. Will
also grow in an indoor case.* 124♦

Above:
Paphiopedilum spiceranum
This is a scarce species that has been popular for many years. It can be grown in the cool to intermediate greenhouse and its flowering period is autumn to winter. Many hybrids have been produced from this distinctive species. It cannot be recommended for beginners. 123◆

Above: **Phalaenopsis Hennessy**
*This outstanding hybrid is for the
warm greenhouse, when its
attractive sprays of flowers can be
produced at various times of the
year. This variety is known as 'Candy
Striped'.* 125♦

Left:
Phalaenopsis lueddemanniana
*This free-flowering species will grow
easily in warm conditions. Beautifully
marked flowers appear in
succession throughout the spring
and summer months. It has been
much used for hybridization.* 125♦

Right: **Phalaenopsis equestris**
*A miniature species for the warm
house or indoor growing case. It is an
extremely free-flowering variety that
blooms mainly during the autumn
and winter months.* 124♦

111

Above: **Phalaenopsis schillerana**
A superb species for the warm greenhouse. It has lovely mottled foliage and bears long pendent sprays of rich pink flowers in the spring. Can be grown in a pot or in a hanging basket to encourage the formation of long aerial roots. 126♦

Odontoglossum pulchellum

- Cool: 10°C (50°F)
- Easy to grow and flower
- Spring flowering
- Evergreen/slight rest

An extremely popular and vigorous Guatemalan species. The waxy, white flowers, though small – 1-2cm (0.4-0.8in) across – bloom in masses and have a lovely scent, which explains why it is known as the 'lily of the valley orchid'. It flowers in spring and produces more than one shoot from each pseudobulb, making it ideal for growing into a specimen. The plants are thin-rooted and need cool conditions, a fine-grade bark mix, and medium shade in the summer.

If left unsupported the slender flower spikes will often assume a pendent position by the time they are in bloom. If an upright position is preferred, the spikes should be lightly tied to thin supporting canes, when the flowers will stand well clear of the foliage. This is an unusual species, which alone among the cultivated odontoglossums carries its flowers with the lip uppermost.

Within the genus, it has not contributed to any hybridization.

It can be easily propagated by the removal of back bulbs. 99♦

Odontoglossum rossii

- Cool: 10°C (50°F)
- Easy to grow and flower
- Winter flowering
- Evergreen/no rest

From Guatemala and Mexico, this is one of the most delightful of the miniature odontoglossums. It is very similar to *Odontoglossum cervantesii* in size of plant and size and colour of flowers, and has similar cultural requirements. The plants are thin-rooted and flourish in cool conditions and a fine bark mix or sphagnum moss that will keep them moist at all times. Medium shade is required during the summer.

A typical variety produces star-shaped flowers in winter, about 3-5cm (1.25-2in) across, white with brown markings; rarer varieties are flushed with pink, or deep pink. Probably the most popular is the Majus variety, which has a much larger flower up to 7.5cm (3in) across. However, this sought after variety is seldom seen today; the smaller forms are usually grown.

Because of their small size, the pseudobulbs should not be allowed to shrivel at any time. During the winter, when the plant is inactive for a short period, watering should be lessened slightly. 98♦

113

Odontoglossum stellatum
- Cool: 10°C (50°F)
- Easy to grow and flower
- Winter flowering
- Evergreen/semi-rest

A dwarf species from Guatemala, this has attractive star-shaped flowers, yellow overlaid with brown, with a white or pink lip. These are usually borne either singly or in pairs during the winter months, but on a specimen plant they are produced in abundance, making a fine display. Each flower measures 3-4cm (1.25-1.5in) across. Found naturally among mosses on branches of trees, this species needs a fine bark mix, with medium shade during the summer; too much light will cause a yellowing of the light green foliage.

Owing to the smallness of the bright green pseudobulbs the plants should not be allowed to dry out completely at any time. During the winter, water should be reduced but not discontinued altogether. Several new growths are produced each season and the plant quickly grows into a good-sized specimen. As it gets larger it should be grown in a half pot, which will allow sufficient room for the fine root system to spread out comfortably without the danger of overwatering.

Oncidium flexuosum
- Cool/intermediate: 10-13°C (50-55°F)
- Easy to grow and flower
- Summer flowering
- Evergreen/short rest

This is a native of Brazil, which is declining in cultivation due to restricted importation. Its light green pseudobulbs arise well spaced out along an upward creeping rhizome, each bulb supporting two light green glossy leaves. Because of its creeping habit it is more easily accommodated on a raft or piece of cork bark, where it will produce an extensive aerial root system forming a dense mat of fine roots 90cm (3ft) across. In such a situation regular overhead spraying is very beneficial.

The flower spikes are produced during the summer. These grow to a length of 90cm (3ft) and end with a branched dense shower of numerous, bright yellow flowers — up to 100 per spike on a large plant. The lip is the largest and most attractive part of the flower, the sepals and petals becoming insignificant. The species propagates easily from back bulbs, which will often start to grow while still attached to the main plant. An ideal plant for beginners.

The plant will need larger pieces of bark as it grows.

Oncidium longipes

- Cool/intermediate:
  10-13°C (50-55°F)
- Easy to grow and flower
- Summer flowering
- Evergreen/no rest

A small-growing species ideal for growing on into a specimen plant in the small greenhouse in cool or intermediate conditions. Short flower spikes carrying three or four flowers, about 2.5cm (1in) across, are produced freely from the base of a small pseudobulb and appear during the summer. They are bright yellow, barred with reddish-brown and have a solid yellow lip.

This Brazilian species is among the most attractive of the smaller-growing oncidiums. Because of its small size it is better not to allow it to become too dry at any time; overhead spraying can be an advantage during the summer. Although the plant will readily divide, to develop its full beauty it should be grown on into a specimen, when it will never become unmanageable.

If new plants are needed then division is the best method of propagation; it is slow to grow from back bulbs. The plant can also be grown on bark, where it will quickly develop into a splendid specimen.

Oncidium ornithorhynchum

- Cool: 10°C (50°F)
- Easy to grow and flower
- Autumn flowering
- Evergreen/semi-rest

An extremely showy species from Mexico and Guatemala, this plant has a compact habit and light green pseudobulbs each topped with several thin leaves. The short, slender and arching flower spikes are produced very freely in the autumn and carry the individual flowers on side branches. These are about 2cm (0.8in) long, the sepals and petals curled and twisted. The colour is a soft rose-lilac with a yellow crest on the lip. They are long-lasting and beautifully fragrant. It is not unusual for two or three flower spikes to be produced by one bulb.

Propagation is by division and removal of back bulbs, although the plant is at its best when grown on into a specimen. A very fine rooting system is produced, indicating that a well-drained compost is important. The plant dislikes cold and damp and should therefore not be sprayed overhead or kept too wet at any time. Otherwise, normal cool house conditions will suit it. It is a delightful beginner's orchid of great charm that will do equally well indoors. 100♦

Oncidium papilio
- **Warm: 18°C (65°F)**
- **Difficult to grow and flower**
- **Varied flowering season**
- **Evergreen/semi-dry rest**

Oncidium tigrinum
- **Cool: 10°C (50°F)**
- **Easy to grow and flower**
- **Autumn flowering**
- **Evergreen/dry rest**

Often referred to as the 'butterfly orchid' because of its resemblance to that insect, this species has flowers that open on the end of a long slender stem and sway in the slightest air movement. Only one per stem opens at any one time, but in succession, so that the plant is in flower for many months. The flowers, which can be up to 13cm (5in) across, are a mixture of chestnut brown and yellow.

The plant has squat pseudobulbs each of which supports a solitary, rigid, reddish-green leaf. The plant grows best on a raft suspended from the roof of the warm house, where it will get that little extra bit of light. It should never be kept too wet at the roots, and does best when kept continually on the dry side, relying upon the humidity in the greenhouse for most of its moisture. It should not be overhead sprayed. This is not a beginner's orchid nor a suitable plant for growing indoors.

Rare in the wild, the plants seen in cultivation have usually been grown from seed. 101♦

Originating from Mexico, this is one of the most beautiful of the autumn flowering oncidiums and certainly one of the most popular. It is a neat, good-looking plant with roundish pseudobubs that each support two or three dark green leaves. The flower spikes can be up to 7.5cm (3in) tall, and branching on a large plant. Several fragrant flowers are carried on each branch as well as on the terminal part of the main stem. The petals and sepals are yellow barred with chocolate brown, and the large, spreading lip is a vivid yellow and by far the most striking part of the flower.

The plant will succeed well in the cool house, although as with many of the Mexican species it will be equally happy in intermediate conditions. The species is becoming less plentiful in cultivation but it has been used to produce some excellent intergeneric crosses within the *Odontoglossum* alliance. Generally these hybrids are tolerant of widely varying conditions and are suitable for most climates.

Paphiopedilum bellatulum
- **Warm: 16-18°C (60-65°F)**
- **Moderately easy to grow**
- **Spring flowering**
- **Evergreen/no rest**

One of the most beautiful of all the species, this native of Burma and Thailand has broad, fleshy leaves that are distinctly mottled and veined with lighter green. As the flower stem is very short, the lovely 6cm (2.5in) flower often nestles in the foliage. The broad, drooping petals are white or ivory, with maroon spots of varying size and density.

Extra care must be taken with its culture to prevent basal rot and other problems that can arise from too much watering or moisture around the plant. It is slow growing by comparison with others of the genus, and the beautiful foliage is easily damaged by unskilled handling. The plant must be grown in as small a pot as possible in a well-drained compost that is kept open and sweet. Water sparingly at all times and do not allow water to remain on the leaves. It will succeed best in a fairly warm greenhouse or in an indoor growing case, with good shade.

This is not an orchid suitable for beginners, who should try the hybrids bred from it.

Paphiopedilum callosum
- **Intermediate: 13°C (55°F)**
- **Easy to grow and flower**
- **Spring/summer flowering**
- **Evergreen/no rest**

This species is a vigorous grower, producing long mottled leaves. The long-lasting flower is borne on a tall stem, up to 38cm (15in) in length, which makes it very popular with the cut flower trade. The flowers are 10cm (4in) across, and coloured in varying shades of purple and green. They will last for eight or ten weeks in perfect condition.

It is a native of Thailand and is still reasonably plentiful in cultivation, no doubt because it can be easily propagated by division of the plants, which can be separated into two or three clumps every few years. The plant is suitable for windowsill culture in a warm room, where it should not be exposed to bright light. Grow in an open compost and water sufficiently to keep the plant evenly moist throughout the year. Keep the foliage dry, although indoors it will be necessary to sponge the leaves regularly to keep them free from dust. The plant may be lightly fed during the spring and summer.

This is an excellent choice for people new to orchid growing.

Paphiopedilum delenatii
- **Intermediate/warm: 13-18°C (55-65°F)**
- **Moderately easy to grow**
- **Summer flowering**
- **Evergreen/no rest**

This species from Vietnam has very dark green, heavily mottled leaves. The flowers, produced in summer and borne on a 20cm (8in) long stem, are 7.5cm (3in) across and soft rose pink in colour. This is one of the few fragrant paphiopedilums.

This plant is a fairly recent introduction and with its neat growth habit and highly attractive, unusual flowers has become justly popular. However, its requirements are rather specialized and it is not ideally suited to the beginner. It has never been very plentiful in the wild, but is easily raised from seed, and excellent young plants are becoming more readily available. It should be kept in as small a pot as possible with just sufficient water to keep it moist; it is intolerant of cold and damp conditions.

Some charming hybrids have also been raised that are proving to be more robust and easily grown. These hybrids would be a better choice for people new to orchids. 104♦

Paphiopedilum fairieanum
- **Cool: 10°C (50°F)**
- **Moderately easy to grow**
- **Winter flowering**
- **Evergreen/no rest**

This very attractive Indian species has an interesting history. It was originally described in 1857 and named in honour of Mr. M. Fairie, in whose collection it flowered. It then became lost to cultivation for many years, and in 1905, when only one small plant existed in England, it was rediscovered after a reward of £1,000 had been offered by Mr. Frederick Sander, a leading orchid nurseryman of his day. From that time the species became very common in cultivation and extremely popular. Today it is once again becoming scarce.

The plant is a modest grower and produces a single flower 6.5cm (2.6in) across. The colouring is mainly purple on a white ground. The dorsal sepal and the petals are heavily striped and the pouch is a dull greenish-purple. The petals turn down and then up, in the fashion of buffalo horns. In recent years the variety *album* was discovered. This lacks any trace of purple and is basically yellow.

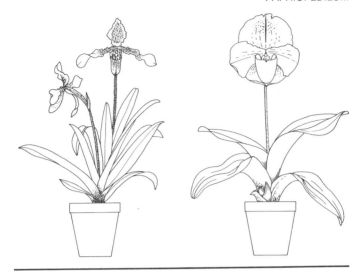

Paphiopedilum hirsutissimum

- **Cool/intermediate: 10-13°C (50-55°F)**
- **Easy to grow and flower**
- **Spring flowering**
- **Evergreen/no rest**

The flowers of this Himalayan species are difficult to describe. They are basically purplish in colour, ranging from blackish-purple in the centre of the flower, to bright violet-purple at the petal tips. The pouch is brownish-purple. The plant gets its name from areas of black hair on the petals.

The plant produces neat green foliage with slender leaves. The flower bud emerges from a sheath that forms as winter approaches. The flowers open in late spring and last for eight weeks or more. The plant grows easily and will succeed in the cool or intermediate sections of the greenhouse. It is also suitable for the windowsill or for a growing case. This plant is at its best when grown on into a large clump, when it will produce several flowers in a season. However, if preferred, it may be divided when large enough; at least three growths should be retained on each plant. The plant should be kept evenly moist throughout the year and not allowed to dry out. 102♦

Paphiopedilum Honey Gorse 'Sunshine'

(AM/RHS)

- **Intermediate: 13°C (55°F)**
- **Easy to grow and flower**
- **Winter flowering**
- **Evergreen/no rest**

The first plant to combine the characteristics of the green and the yellow paphiopedilum groups, the 10cm (4in) flowers of this hybrid are dark yellow-green. Deeper emerald green hybrids are now being bred, but this plant will take some beating for its heavy texture – a feature usually lacking in the green colour group.

The plant contrasts beautifully with the heavier coloured and spotted flowers in the other colour ranges. It offers the grower a clear, fresh alternative to enhance any collection.

The plant should be repotted annually to ensure fresh, free-draining compost while keeping the pot size as small as possible. An intermediate greenhouse will suit this hybrid type best, where shady conditions should prevail. These hybrids are usually slower growing than many of the species and therefore splitting is not normally recommended unless or until the plant has several large growths. 105♦

Paphiopedilum insigne
- **Cool: 10°C (50°F)**
- **Easy to grow and flower**
- **Winter flowering**
- **Evergreen/no rest**

Paphiopedilum Maudiae
- **Intermediate: 13°C (55°F)**
- **Easy to grow and flower**
- **Varied flowering season**
- **Evergreen/no rest**

One of the orchid 'greats', this plant has enjoyed unwavering popularity since it was first flowered in 1820. It is a native of the Himalayas and produces stocky, well-leafed growths that bloom freely in mid-winter, lasting for many weeks in perfection. The dorsal (uppermost) sepal is green with a white tip and spotted dark brown. The petals and pouch are bronze, the petals veined along their length. Among numerous varieties is the pure yellow type, *P. insigne* var. *sanderae.*

Today, though still popular, these beautiful orchids are dwindling in cultivation due to the difficulties of importing from the wild. What was, up to a few years ago, a desirable beginner's orchid is now becoming a rare collector's item. However, it will never be lost to cultivation as it will propagate easily and can be nursery raised from seed. Used extensively in hybridizing, there is hardly a modern *Paphiopedilum* hybrid that cannot trace back to this species. Beginners should try the hybrids. 103♦

This is probably the most consistently popular *Paphiopedilum* hybrid in the world. The plant has the grace and beauty found among a few of the species, which have been overshadowed by the heavier, rounded type of hybrids. This hybrid results from a cross of *Paph. callosum* x *Paph. lawrenceanum,* using two green varieties.

The plant is a strong, vigorous grower that can be continually divided without harm to produce further plants. The foliage is beautifully mottled in light and dark green, the leaves are short and rounded. The tall, slender stem carries a single large bloom, distinctively marked in white and deep apple green. Its coloured variety, *Paph.* Maudiae 'Coloratum', shows the same markings on a rich purple ground.

Its ease of culture and long-lasting, long-stemmed blooms, which can be produced twice in one year, have made this hybrid popular for the cut flower trade. 104♦

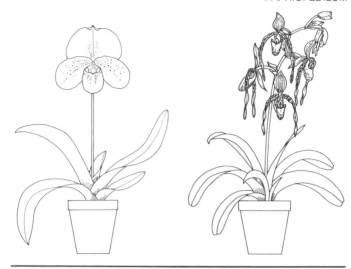

Paphiopedilum Miller's Daughter 'Snow Maiden'
- Intermediate: 13°C (55°F)
- Easy to grow and flower
- Winter flowering
- Evergreen/no rest

This line represents the most advanced breeding for white-flowered hybrids in the world. There is nothing to compare with the perfection of the Miller's Daughter hybrids for flower size, shape and vigour. The 13cm (5in) flowers of this particular plant (*P.* Dusty Miller 'Mary' AM/RHS & GMM x *P.* Chantal 'Aloha') are white, lightly speckled all over with pinkish-brown.

The plant will succeed best in an intermediate greenhouse under moist, shady conditions. It should never be allowed to become completely dry at any time. Having no pseudobulbs in which to store water, its meagre reserves are held in the leaves; and if dryness is permitted, the foliage will become limp and dehydrated. The same symptoms will occur if overwatering has taken place; the roots drown in the sodden compost and the plant is deprived of its method of taking up water.

This lovely plant flowers during the winter months of the year. 107♦

Paphiopedilum parishii
- Intermediate: 13°C (55°F)
- Moderately easy to grow
- Winter flowering
- Evergreen/no rest

A very striking species from Burma and Thailand that often grows epiphytically. The long narrow leaves are very smooth and bright glossy green. The erect flower stem, which can grow to 60cm (24in) in height, bears four to seven flowers, each about 7.5cm (3in) across, from autumn to spring. The twisted petals are long and pendulous, purplish-brown in overall colour, and spotted towards the flower centre. The pouch is greenish-brown, and the dorsal sepal greenish-yellow.

It does not require a great deal of light to flower, but will only bloom when mature. For this reason it should be grown without division. It is one of the very few paphiopedilums which produce a spray of flowers that open all at the same time on the stem. To keep the foliage clean and unmarked avoid allowing water to remain on the surface of the leaves, and be careful not to give too much light. This applies particularly to bright spring sunshine. 106♦

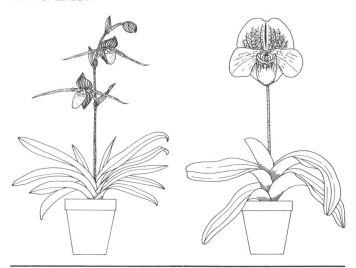

Paphiopedilum rothschildanum

- Intermediate: 13°C (55°F)
- Moderately easy to grow
- Summer/autumn flowering
- Evergreen/no rest

This species from New Guinea is one of the most striking paphiopedilums. The straight, leathery leaves are bright glossy green and can measure up to 60cm (24in) in length. The long flower stem carries two to five flowers, which can be as much as 29cm (11.5in) across. The flower markings are complicated, the overall colour being cinnamon yellow to greenish-brown, with dark brown stripes on the long petals and pointed dorsal sepal.

This plant is rarely seen today in collections. Those plants which are in cultivation are usually held as breeding stock. This ensures that it will never become extinct, and nursery raised seedlings or hybrids from it can occasionally be found. It is not really a beginner's orchid but the species or its hybrids are desirable collector's plants. Most suitable for an intermediate greenhouse, it will enjoy shady conditions in a moist atmosphere.

It should not be divided too often, but allowed to grow on. 103♦

Paphiopedilum Royale 'Downland'

(AM/RHS & GMM)
- Intermediate: 13°C (55°F)
- Easy to grow and flower
- Winter flowering
- Evergreen/no rest

This hybrid is a seedling from the illustrious *P.* Paeony 'Regency' (AM/RHS) line, and has very large flowers, 15cm (6in) across, borne on long flower spikes. The flowers, which are an interesting colour combination of soft rose-red shaded with green, open in the winter.

The plant should be grown in the intermediate greenhouse, under warm and shady conditions with an even moisture. Annual repotting is recommended to maintain the compost in a fresh and open condition and thus ensure a steady rate of growth. When in bloom, these heavy flowers will need the support of a thin bamboo cane and green string tie, or a thin wire stake. The blooms will last for up to ten weeks on the plant, after which the stem should be cut and the plant encouraged to make its new growth for the following season.

This plant can be recommended for beginners to orchid growing provided a warm and shady position is available for it to thrive. 107♦

Paphiopedilum spiceranum

- **Cool/intermediate: 10-13°C (50-55°F)**
- **Moderately easy to grow**
- **Autumn/winter flowering**
- **Evergreen/no rest**

A native of Assam, this species has broad leaves with wavy margins, dark green above and spotted with purple underneath. In autumn and winter one or two 7.5cm (3in) flowers are borne on a 30cm (12in) stem. They are distinctive in markings and shape and play an important role in the breeding of hybrids. One notable feature of the otherwise bronze flower is the hooded white dorsal sepal, which carries a central purple stripe, a feature it has passed on to many of its hybrids.

An accommodating orchid, it will grow successfully in a cool or intermediate greenhouse, or in similar conditions indoors. This is a scarce species and good plants may be difficult to acquire. It is not as easy to grow as some *Paphiopedilum* species and should not be attempted by the beginner, who would do better to try a hybrid from it. The plant should be given shady conditions and kept moist all the year round with occasional light overhead spraying for good measure. 108♦

Paphiopedilum venustum

- **Intermediate: 13°C (55°F)**
- **Easy to grow and flower**
- **Spring flowering**
- **Evergreen/no rest**

The leaves of this species are heavily marbled with grey and green. One or, occasionally, two flowers, 7.5cm (3in) across, are borne on a 15-23cm (6-9in) stem. The petals and lip are basically yellow-green, tinged with rose-red, and the petals are slightly hairy. The dorsal sepal is white, strongly striped with green. The plant blooms in early spring.

This is an excellent choice for the intermediate greenhouse. The neat plant is attractive in and out of flower. The delightful flowers are showy and long-lasting. The species comes from the Himalayas and should be given shady conditions with a good fresh atmosphere. Regular repotting will ensure that the compost remains fresh and free-draining. This species, though still reasonably plentiful, has not been used in breeding new hybrids as extensively as a number of other paphiopedilums, and its influence is not noticeable in most of today's modern hybrids. An easy plant to grow and flower. 108♦

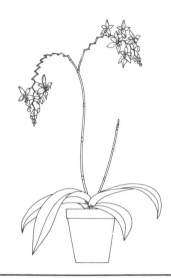

Phalaenopsis Barbara Moler

- Warm: 18-21°C (65-70°F)
- Easy to grow and flower
- Spring/autumn flowering
- Evergreen/no rest

P. Barbara Moler is a comparatively compact grower, with leaves some 30cm (12in) long and 10cm (4in) wide. The flower spikes, which are long – up to 46cm (18in) – and branched, bear flowers for many months from spring to autumn. Individually, the flowers are 7cm (2.75in) across, and of very heavy texture. There are two colour forms. The best-known is white with heavy pink spotting, giving an overall appearance of rich pink. The second form can best be described as yellow; the base colour is greenish-yellow overlaid with yellow-chestnut blotches.

P. Barbara Moler is already proving to be a very important parent in breeding for heavy texture and new colour breaks. *P.* Space Queen is an example of the type of hybrid produced from *P.* Barbara Moler breeding.

This plant thrives in warm, shady conditions and should be kept evenly moist throughout the year. It should not be grown in too large a pot for the size of the plant. 108♦

Phalaenopsis equestris

- Warm: 18-21°C (65-70°F)
- Easy to grow and flower
- Autumn/winter flowering
- Evergreen/no rest

This species is said to be the commonest phalaenopsis of the Philippines. The plant is comparatively compact in growth and has leathery, dull green leaves some 15cm (6in) long and 7.5cm (3in) wide. The very graceful arching flower spikes bear pale rose flowers, 2.5cm (1in) across, with a darker oval lip. The flowers open in autumn and winter.

P. equestris was used as a parent to produce the first manmade hybrid phalaenopsis, *P.* Artemis, in 1892. It still plays a part in modern hybridizing where compact, small-flowered plants are in demand.

This plant is suitable for a warm greenhouse, or being a compact grower, it will be easily accommodated in an indoor growing case. It can be grown in a pot or, with equal success, in a basket, or it can be mounted on bark for hanging in a shady place. Exposure to full sun will quickly scorch the tough leathery foliage. It should be kept evenly moist throughout the year and lightly sprayed in summer. 111♦

Phalaenopsis Hennessy
- **Warm: 18-21°C (65-70°F)**
- **Easy to grow and flower**
- **Varied flowering season**
- **Evergreen/no rest**

This hybrid is an example of a peppermint-striped phalaenopsis. The plant is very free-flowering, blooming throughout the year, and the branched spikes may bear up to 30 flowers at a time. The individual flowers are 9-12cm (3.5-4.75in) across, white to light pink in basic colour, with red or pink stripes or, in some forms, spots. The lip varies in colour from deep rosy pink to orange.

This hybrid type is of fairly recent breeding, and the plants are in limited supply. From a particular cross, only a percentage of the seedlings will carry the elusive candy-striped markings that are highly valued to increase the variety within the genus. *Phalaenopsis* flowers are highly susceptible to damp conditions, when premature spotting of the flowers will occur. A movement of air from an electric fan combined with a drier atmosphere while the plants are in bloom will help to prevent this common problem. The plants will also suffer if given poor light during the winter. 110♦

Phalaenopsis lueddemanniana
- **Warm: 18-21°C (65-70°F)**
- **Easy to grow and flower**
- **Spring/summer flowering**
- **Evergreen/no rest**

This free-flowering species is easy to grow and one of the most variable of the *Phalaenopsis* genus. The leaves are usually light green, broad and long. The flower spikes, several of which may be produced at the same time, each carry 20 or so 2.5cm (1in) flowers that open in succession throughout spring and summer. The sepals and petals are white or yellow, marked with bars or spots ranging from pink to deep purple, and the small lip is usually purple. If the plant is given cooler and more shady conditions when the first buds appear, richer colours will be produced. The flower spikes readily produce plantlets at their nodes.

The species has been widely used in breeding with great success, two of the best-known hybrids from *P. lueddemanniana* being *P.* Golden Sands and *P.* Cabrillo Star. As the name suggests, *P.* Golden Sands is a fine yellow hybrid, and *P.* Cabrillo Star is a large white bloom heavily spotted with red.

It likes warm, shady conditions. 110♦

Phalaenopsis schillerana

- **Warm: 18-21°C (65-70°F)**
- **Easy to grow and flower**
- **Spring flowering**
- **Evergreen/no rest**

The best-known phalaenopsis, and held in great esteem. It was discovered in Manila in 1858 growing on trees, often very high up. The plants fix themselves to the branches and trunks by numerous flattened roots. In cultivation these roots grow to considerable lengths along any firm surface within their reach, and are almost impossible to release without breaking. As they mature they develop a beautiful silver sheen.

As a decorative plant, *P. schillerana* is hard to beat; the handsome leaves, up to 46cm (18in) or more in length, are deep green, marbled and blotched with grey and silver. The flowers, 5-7.5cm (2-3in) across, of a delicate rose purple, are often borne in great numbers during early spring on a branched arching spike, which may grow to 90cm (3ft) in length.

The plant has been used extensively in breeding and is responsible for producing many of the fine pink hybrids that are available today. 112♦

Phalaenopsis Space Queen

- **Warm: 18-21°C (65-70°F)**
- **Easy to grow and flower**
- **Varied flowering season**
- **Evergreen/no rest**

Crossing *P.* Barbara Moler with *P.* Temple Cloud has produced this hybrid with beautiful flowers of heavy substance, 9-10cm (3.5-4in) across, soft pink or white, heavily spotted with red.

This plant is a strong, robust grower which, when grown to perfection, can be expected to bloom twice a year. *Phalaenopsis* plants must not be allowed to get cold, and if the minimum recommended temperature of 18°C (65°F) or, better still, 21°C (70°F) cannot be maintained easily throughout the winter, it is better not to attempt to grow them. These beautiful orchids should be given a warm section on their own. In these conditions they are not difficult to grow, and most of the cultural problems encountered are the result of insufficient heat. Even when grown in pots, *Phalaenopsis* will make a number of long aerial roots that will meander along the staging for up to 90cm (3ft). Wherever possible these roots should be left undisturbed. 129♦

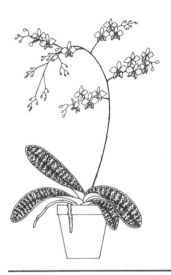 

Phalaenopsis stuartiana

- **Warm: 18-21°C (65-70°F)**
- **Easy to grow and flower**
- **Spring flowering**
- **Evergreen/no rest**

This species is very similar to *P. schillerana,* and when not in flower they are virtually impossible to tell apart: the foliage is the same deep green, marbled in grey and silver, and the roots have the same flattened appearance. In the wild it is said to be found always closely associated with water, sometimes close to the shoreline, where the plants are subjected to salt-water spray.

The spike habit and quantity of flowers are also like those of *P. schillerana,* but in *P. stuartiana* the upper sepal and two side petals are white. Of the two lower sepals one half is white and the other heavily spotted with reddish-purple; the orange-yellow lip is also spotted. The overall appearance when in flower is thus distinct and striking.

Many hybrids have been registered from this species, all showing the characteristic spotting, and it is valuable for introducing orange shades to the lip when crossed with white hybrids.

Thrives in warmth and shade. 129♦

Phalaenopsis Temple Cloud

- **Warm: 18°C (65°F)**
- **Easy to grow and flower**
- **Varied flowering season**
- **Evergreen/no rest**

Resulting from the crossing of two outstanding hybrids, *P.* Opaline and *P.* Keith Shaffer, this hybrid took on the finer points of both parents, producing pure white 11.5cm (4.5in) round blooms of heavy texture, and in turn proved to be a very successful parent. It can be in flower at any season.

Like all the other modern *Phalaenopsis* hybrids it is not difficult to grow and can be in bloom for months at a time provided it is given plenty of warmth. This important factor makes it ideal for growing in an indoor case, where the high temperatures required can be more easily achieved. It is a shade-loving or low light plant, which enables it to be successfully grown and flowered in artificial light conditions. The plant should be grown in as small a pot as possible, in a free-draining bark compost. It should be fed at every third watering for most of the year, and never be allowed to dry out completely.

The flowers can be cut and used for flower arrangements. 131♦

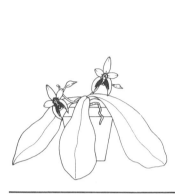

Phalaenopsis violacea
- **Warm: 18-21°C (65-70°F)**
- **Moderately easy to grow**
- **Summer flowering**
- **Evergreen/no rest**

First discovered in 1859, this species has two distinct types, one from Borneo, the other from Malaya. Although it may not be the easiest species to maintain in good flowering condition, it is nevertheless very attractive, as it combines beauty with fragrance. The 7.5cm (3in) flowers of the Borneo type have the fragrance of violets and are borne in summer on a short pendulous spike, often in succession. The flowers of the Malaysian form are smaller and of a fuller shape, about 6.5cm (2.6in) across. The plant requires deep shade and high humidity.

The first hybrid, *P. violacea* x *P. amabilis,* was registered by James Veitch in 1887 as *P.* Harrietiae. In recent years, *P. violacea* has been used extensively in breeding, with great success.

Today, this plant is practically unobtainable from the wild. However, selected varieties are being raised from seed and these young plants are more easily grown than wild imports.

Thrives in warmth and shade. 130♦

Pleione formosana
- **Very cool: 4.5°C (40°F)**
- **Easy to grow and flower**
- **Spring flowering**
- **Evergreen/dry rest**

Until recently orchid growers had not taken this genus seriously, unlike the alpine growers, who cultivate pleiones with great success. The 20 known species are found growing close to the snowline of the Himalayas, and also in parts of China and Formosa. The Himalayan species are probably better suited to the conditions of an alpine house, but others do well in the cool section of an orchid house.

The plant consists of a single, squat, roundish pseudobulb, which lasts for only one year. New growth springs from the base of the pseudobulb, and in its early stages produces a flower spike from its centre. This spike bears one or two flowers, up to 10cm (4in) across. The common species has flowers ranging from pure white to pale pinky-mauve. In all variations the broad lip is frilled, and in the coloured forms it is spotted with red-purple.

In the early spring the plants should be taken from their pot, and reset about half-buried in a fine but well-draining compost. 131♦

Above:
Phalaenopsis Space Queen
*Large flowers are produced on long
sprays at various times. This modern
hybrid thrives in warm conditions.* 126♦

Below: **Phalaenopsis stuartiana**
*Tall, branching flower sprays are
produced in the spring. A lovely
warm-house species much used for
hybridization.* 127♦

Above: **Phalaenopsis violacea**
This warm-house species flowers in the summer. It produces solitary flowers which are very striking, fragrant and long lasting. Many hybrids are being produced from it and these contain much of the rich colouring seen here in the lower sepals. 128♦

Above right:
Phalaenopsis Temple Cloud
A pure white hybrid for the warm house. Varied flowering times. 127♦

Right: **Pleione formosana**
Will grow very cool in an alpine house. Flowers in the spring and is deciduous during the winter. 128♦

Above: **Pleione formosana var. alba 'Snow White'**
These spring flowers will last for two to three weeks on the plant. 145♦

Above: **Rhynchostylis retusa**
Long dense sprays of small flowers adorn this intermediate species during the winter and spring. 147♦

Left: **Saccolabium acutifolium**
This autumn-flowering species will grow particularly well mounted on bark in the intermediate house. 147♦

Below: **Potinara Sunrise**
A lovely Cattleya type hybrid for autumn flowering in the intermediate house. Fragrant blooms. 146♦

Above: **Polystachya pubescens**
*A small-growing, unusual species
for the intermediate house. It blooms
at various times of the year.* 145♦

Right: **Stanhopea tigrina**
*Magnificent but short-lived summer
flowers. A highly fragrant species.
Grow cool in a basket.* 149♦

Below: **Sobralia macrantha**
*A tall-growing species for fairly cool
conditions. Summer flowering.
Flowers are short-lived and are
produced in succession.* 148♦

Far left: Stanhopea wardii
This highly fragrant summer-flowering species is cool growing. Flowers last just a few days, and emerge from beneath the plant, which is best grown in a basket. 149♦

Left: Sophronitis coccinea
Charming flowers appear on this miniature epiphytic orchid during late winter or spring. A plant for cool or intermediate conditions, it can prove difficult to maintain. 148♦

Below: Vanda coerulea
This blue-flowered species is for the intermediate house. Sprays of lovely flowers are produced during the autumn months of the year. A rare collector's item. 150♦

Above: **Trichopilia tortilis**
A summer-flowering species of compact habit for the cool or intermediate greenhouse. 150♦

Below: **Vanda cristata**
A small-growing species for cool or intermediate conditions. It blooms in the spring and summer. 151♦

Above: **Vanda Onomea 'Walcrest'**
This Vanda hybrid is a warm-house plant that requires good light to grow and flower well. The large blooms appear in the summer and are carried on many-flowered stems. These orchids are not really suitable for the beginner. 153♦

Above: **Vanda Nelly Morley**
This sun-loving, warm-house hybrid produces its sprays of large colourful flowers at various times. 152♦

Left: **Vanda Jennie Hashimoto 'Starles'**
A free-flowering hybrid for the warm house. It will bloom under sunny conditions in the summer. 151♦

Below: **Vanda sanderana**
This rare species is suitable for the warm-house. It blooms during the summer and needs sunlight to grow and flower well. 154♦

Above left: **Vanda Rothschildiana**
This warm-growing, winter-flowering hybrid is easier to grow than most Vanda *hybrids.* 153♦

Left: **Vanda Thonglor**
An outstanding hybrid for the warm greenhouse. It normally flowers during the summer months. 155♦

Above: **Vanda suavis**
A tall-growing species for the warm house. It flowers freely in the autumn and winter on long fragrant sprays. This is a sun-loving species that also requires a high humidity. It is an orchid for the specialist who can give it the necessary culture. Also found under the name Vanda tricolor. 154♦

Right: **Wilsonara Widecombe Fair**
An easy-to-grow, cool-house hybrid that produces hundreds of flowers on a long branching spike. 156♦

Below: **Vuylstekeara Cambria 'Plush'**
Cool- or intermediate-growing, variable flowering. Very easy. 155♦

Bottom:
Zygopetalum intermedium
A fragrant, winter-flowering species for the intermediate house. Often known as Zygopetalum mackayi. 156♦

(Shown in full summer growth.)

Pleione formosana variety alba 'Snow White'
- **Very cool: 4.5°C (40°F)**
- **Easy to grow and flower**
- **Spring flowering**
- **Evergreen/dry rest**

This is the white variety of the popular and very cool-growing species. Unlike the common species the single flowers on this variety have pure white, glistening petals and sepals, and the lip is lightly spotted. It is a charming orchid to grow, and one that requires the least heat of any in cultivation. During the summer, normal cool house conditions will suit. While at rest during the winter it should be kept as cool as possible. The plants make ideal windowsill orchids and are easy for beginners.

When the flower has died away, a pseudobulb develops at the base of the new growth and the parent pseudobulb shrivels. The new growth should be complete by the late autumn, when the broad but fairly short leaves turn yellow and drop. The pseudobulbs should then be stored for the winter in a cool dry place. Watering should start in the spring, sparingly at first.

Several bulbs planted in one pot will produce a good show. 133♦

Polystachya pubescens
- **Intermediate: 13°C (55°F)**
- **Easy to grow and flower**
- **Varied flowering season**
- **Evergreen/no rest**

The majority of the 150 known species of *Polystachya* come from tropical Africa. Though the flowers are generally small, the plants flower freely under cultivation.

These plants are subjects for the intermediate house. Being epiphytic, they require a well-drained compost, but plenty of moisture at the root while the plant is in active growth. Moderate protection from the full sun is also required. Polystachyas undoubtedly do best when left undisturbed for several years.

A notable feature is that the flowers appear upside-down on the spike, the lip being uppermost with the two sepals, normally at the base of the flower, forming a hood.

This species produces narrow, tapering pseudobulbs, which grow to a height of 5cm (2in) and have two or three short leaves. The flower spike comes from the apex of the pseudobulb and carries six to 12 bright yellow flowers, each up to 1.5cm (0.6in) across, the upper sepals and lip of which are marked delicately with red lines. 134♦

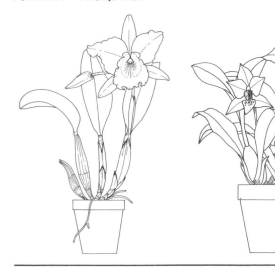

Potinara Sunrise

- **Intermediate: 13°C (55°F)**
- **Easy to grow and flower**
- **Autumn flowering**
- **Evergreen/some rest**

With colourful magenta flowers and slightly darker lips, this hybrid is the result of a quadrigeneric cross (*Brassavola* x *Cattleya* x *Laelia* x *Sophronitis*). The flowers, which open in the autumn, are 13-15cm (5-6in) across and very showy.

Generally, the flowers of potinaras are of a slightly heavier texture, with better lasting qualities. The flowers will become prematurely spotted, however, in over-moist conditions. As with all cattleya hybrids, it is advisable to keep the plants and their surroundings on the dry side while the plants are flowering.

Repotting may be carried out after flowering in the autumn or later in the spring. The aim should be to catch the new growths when they are about 2.5cm (1in) long, just before the new roots appear. All intergeneric cattleyas do well when grown in good light and when given a rest after flowering until the new growth starts.

During the summer these plants can be lightly sprayed overhead, but the foliage should be dry well before nightfall. 133◗

Promenaea xanthina

- **Intermediate: 13°C (55°F)**
- **Easy to grow and flower**
- **Summer flowering**
- **Evergreen/no rest**

This species is alternatively named *P. citrina* and is identical vegetatively to *P. stapelioides*. The flowers are citron yellow in colour with a few tiny red spots on the lip.

Although there are only about 12 recorded species of this Brazilian genus, only two or three of which are found in present-day collections, it is nevertheless popular with orchid growers because the plants are short and compact and produce many flowers. They are ideal subjects for growing on into specimen plants.

The plants are epiphytic and grow best in intermediate conditions, with heavy shade during the summer months. They are intolerant of stale conditions at the root and, ideally, should be repotted in well-draining compost every year.

In both species the flowers appear during the summer and are long-lasting, remaining in good condition for up to six weeks if kept cool.

The foliage should be kept dry at all times and not sprayed from overhead for fear of causing a basal rot in the plant.

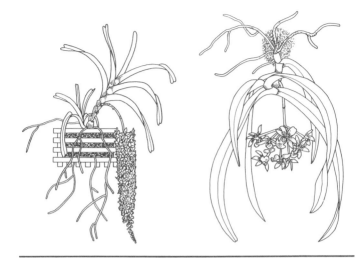

Rhynchostylis retusa
- **Intermediate: 13°C (55°F)**
- **Easy to grow and flower**
- **Winter/spring flowering**
- **Evergreen/no rest**

Four species make up this well-known and popular epiphytic genus, and all are seen in present-day collections.

Their natural habitat is Malaysia and Indonesia and, consequently, they enjoy reasonably warm conditions, similar to those of the strap-leaf vandas, which they resemble vegetatively. Because the flowers grow densely in cylindrical fashion on a pendent raceme or spike, they are commonly known as 'foxtail orchids', although this name is also given to other orchids that produce their flowers in similar fashion (eg *Aerides fieldingii*).

This species produces a plant up to 60cm (2ft) in height with a pendulous spike of 38-50cm (15-20in) which carries many thick, waxy and highly fragrant flowers, each up to 2cm (0.8in) in diameter. These are basically white but may be lightly or heavily spotted with magenta-purple. The hook-shaped lip is solid magenta. The flowers appear from winter to spring and last for only two or three weeks, but if well grown the plant will flower more often. 133♦

Saccolabium acutifolium
- **Intermediate: 13°C (55°F)**
- **Easy to grow and flower**
- **Autumn flowering**
- **Evergreen/no rest**

This species belongs to a small epiphytic group of about 20 species. It originates from India and is now more correctly *Gastrochilus acutifolius,* although the older name persists in horticulture. The plant produces upward growing (monopodial) stems from which grow the narrow, pointed leaves. The fragrant flowers come from between the leaves and are carried on a short, pendent stem in the form of a rosette. These are highly variable and can be pure yellow-green, shaded with brown to an almost solid red colouring. The lip is of curious shape, basically white, occasionally spotted in red with a central yellow stain, and frilled around the edge. It is the shape of the lip that gives the genus *Gastrochilus* its name: *gaster* (belly) and *cheilos* (lip).

The plant will grow happily on a piece of bark in a pendent position, when it will produce a number of dangling aerial roots. It should be kept permanently moist and prefers to be grown in fairly heavy shade. During the summer months it can be sprayed generously. 132♦

Sobralia macrantha
- **Cool/intermediate:**
  10-13°C (50-55°F)
- **Easy to grow and flower**
- **Summer flowering**
- **Evergreen/semi-rest**

This genus contains 30 to 35 very
handsome species, most of which
are indigenous to tropical America.
They are terrestrial plants producing
long, slender, reed-like stems up to
2.4m (8ft) tall, although they are
usually much shorter under
cultivation. Leaves are produced
along almost the full length of the
stem.

The flowers, which are produced
from the apex of the stems, are very
similar in shape and general form to
those of cattleyas. They last for only
two or three days, but to compensate
for this there is a quick succession of
blooms from each stem, and a plant
with a number of leads can be in
flower for many weeks. The flowers
are 13-15cm (5-6in) across, deep or
pale purplish-mauve, with a yellow
throat to the lip.

Sobralias like plenty of sunshine
and fresh air. During the growing
season they must be kept very moist
at the root, whereas when the plant
is at rest, over the winter months, it
should be kept drier, but never
allowed to dry out. They can be
overhead sprayed in summer. 134♦

Sophronitis coccinea
- **Cool/intermediate:**
  10-13°C (50-55°F)
- **Moderately easy to grow**
- **Varied flowering season**
- **Evergreen/no rest**

Although only six species of this
miniature epiphytic orchid are
known, all of which come from Brazil,
it has always been well represented
in orchid collections, and its alliance
with cattleyas has produced some of
the most striking of the intergeneric
hybrids.

In their natural habitat these plants
grow mainly in areas of high humidity
and shade, and therefore are
subjects for the cool or intermediate
house, with good shade during the
summer months. They seem to grow
best on a piece of cork bark, but they
will also grow in a pot. Perfect
drainage at the root is essential.
Unfortunately, even in ideal
conditions, sophronitis plants seem
to have a lifespan of only a few years.

Formerly known as *S. grandiflora,*
this orchid is vegetatively similar to a
tiny cattleya, growing no higher than
7.5cm (3in). The single flower,
6.5cm (2.6in) across, is produced on
a short stem that grows from the top
of the pseudobulb. The petals are
broader than the sepals and all the
segments are bright scarlet, with the
lip marked or lined with yellow. 137♦

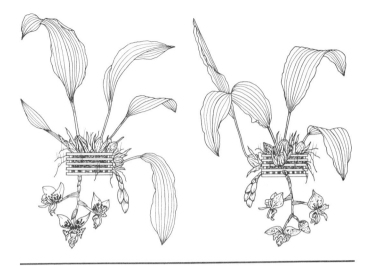

Stanhopea tigrina
- Cool/intermediate:
  10-13°C (50-55°F)
- Easy to grow and flower
- Summer flowering
- Evergreen/dry rest

About 25 species of this fascinating genus have been described, although some may be variants rather than species. They are particularly remarkable for both their growth habit and their unusual flower shape. All are epiphytic and come from tropical America.

The flowering habit of stanhopeas is unusual in that the flower spike, which develops from the base of the pseudobulb, grows directly downwards through the compost to flower beneath the plant. For this reason, these orchids must be grown in wire or wooden-slatted baskets. Unfortunately, these highly fragrant flowers last for only about three days; nevertheless, the plants are of enormous interest and worthy of a place in any mixed collection of orchids.

The flowers of this species tend to be larger than those of *S. wardii*. The basic colour is ivory or pale yellow, and the sepals and petals are heavily blotched with maroon-purple. It is easily the most striking species and very fragrant. A large plant will bloom very freely in succession. 135♦

Stanhopea wardii
- Cool/intermediate:
  10-13°C (50-55°F)
- Easy to grow and flower
- Summer flowering
- Evergreen/dry rest

In common with the other species, *Stanhopea wardii* produces a 30-38cm (12-15in) broad, leathery leaf from the top of an oval pseudobulb. The flower spike, when it has emerged from the plant container, carries three to nine flowers in late summer. The buds develop very quickly and the flowers, up to 10cm (4in) across when fully open, vary from pale lemon to orange, dotted with brownish-purple, with a large blotch of the same colour on each side of the lip. The very strange shape of these flowers suggests a large insect hovering in flight.

Stanhopeas are among the easiest orchids to grow, requiring the conditions of the cool to intermediate house with moderate shade and moisture at the roots at all times. They should be grown in baskets or in purpose-made pots that have holes in the walls and base to prevent the flowers being trapped within the container. A large plant will bloom freely; the spikes open in succession, greatly extending the flowering season. 136♦

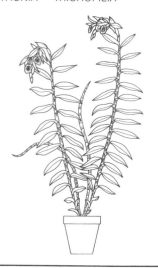

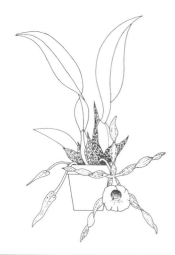

Thunia alba
- Cool/intermediate:
  10-13°C (50-55°F)
- Moderately easy to grow
- Summer flowering
- Evergreen/dry rest

This plant belongs to a small genus of about eight species which are very decorative but seldom seen in cultivation. They are usually terrestrial, occasionally semi-epiphytic plants that originate from India. Tall, straight pseudobulbs (canes) are produced up to 60cm (2ft) high. The soft, blue-green leaves are narrow and pointed and produced from sheaths the length of the canes. The flowers appear from the apex of the cane as it approaches maturity. The large, drooping cluster carries four to six flowers, each 6cm (2.4in) across. These are glistening white, the hairy lip densely marked with yellow and some brown spots.

Annual repotting is recommended. Intermediate conditions will suit in summer, but avoid wetting the foliage and feed liberally. The leaves will turn yellow and drop off as winter approaches, when a cool, dry rest in full light is required. The canes can be removed from their pot and laid on the greenhouse rafters to ripen. Extra feed in the form of old dried cow manure can be used in repotting.

Trichopilia tortilis
- Cool/intermediate:
  10-13°C (50-55°F)
- Easy to grow and flower
- Summer flowering
- Evergreen/semi-rest

About 30 species of *Trichopilia* are known, although only a few of these are available to growers today. Despite this, they remain very popular, partly because they are not difficult to cultivate and also because of their very showy flowers, which are large in comparison with the size of the plant. The plants are epiphytic and are found mainly in South America.

The plants, which never grow very tall, develop flattened pseudobulbs that may be rounded or elongated, and a solitary leathery leaf. Intermediate house conditions suit them well, with good shade during the summer months. The plants benefit from generous moisture at the root in full growth. After flowering, these orchids should be allowed a period of semi-rest.

This plant carries a single flower, up to 13cm (5in) across, on a pendent spike. The sepals and petals, which are narrow and twisted throughout their length, are brown, bordered by a narrow yellow-green band; the trumpet-shaped lip is white with some rose-red spotting. 138♦

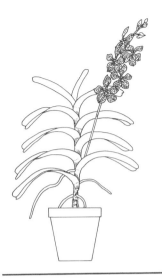

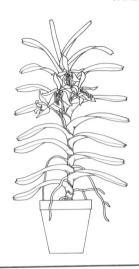

Vanda coerulea
- **Intermediate: 13°C (55°F)**
- **Moderately easy to grow**
- **Autumn/winter flowering**
- **Evergreen/semi-rest**

This is perhaps the showiest and most popular vanda for collectors. Blooming in autumn and winter with lovely pale blue flowers, *V. coerulea* is found wild in the Himalayas, Burma and Thailand, growing at about 1,220-1,830m (approx. 4,000-6,000ft). The leaves are leathery and rigid, about 25cm (10in) long and 2.5cm (1in) wide, and the flower stems are erect or arching to about 60cm (2ft) with from five to 20 flowers per spike.

The flowers can be variable in colour, shape and size, but are generally 10cm (4in) across with pale blue sepals and petals and a network of darker markings. The lip is purple-blue marked with white. Though most vandas revel in warmth, *V. coerulea* is a subject for the intermediate greenhouse.

Today this plant is seldom seen in collections owing to its rarity. Imported plants are no longer available and it is to the nurseryman that you should look for supplies of nursery-raised seedlings. These are not plentiful as the species is not easy to raise from seed. 137♦

Vanda cristata
- **Cool/intermediate: 10-13°C (50-55°F)**
- **Easy to grow and flower**
- **Spring/summer flowering**
- **Evergreen/semi-rest**

This small orchid, which grows only to about 25cm (10in), is a good subject for indoor growing. It is native to high-altitude areas of Nepal and Bhutan. The leaves are 15cm (6in) long and the flowers waxy and fragrant, about 5cm (2in) across. The sepals and petals are mostly yellow-green, and the entire flower is marked with blood-red longitudinal stripes and spots. Blooming from early spring until mid-summer, this is a fine orchid for those with limited space.

This species is one of the few vandas suitable for beginners. It flowers very freely on a modestly sized plant and the flowers last for many weeks. Regular spraying of the whole plant, except when in bloom, will encourage the growth of fat, aerial roots, which grow at right angles from the stem. When the green tips of the roots become concealed by a white covering the plant is at rest and should be kept semi-dry.

This plant enjoys a position of good light in the cool or intermediate greenhouse. 138♦

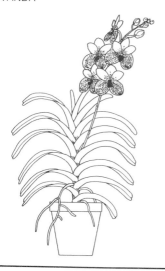

Vanda Jennie Hashimoto 'Starles'
- **Warm: 18°C (65°F)**
- **A challenge to grow**
- **Summer flowering**
- **Evergreen/no rest**

Vanda Nelly Morley
- **Warm: 18°C (65°F)**
- **A challenge to grow**
- **Varied flowering season**
- **Evergreen/no rest**

A recent cross between *V. sanderana* and *V.* Onomea that shows good flower form and is becoming popular with collectors. In the summer, mature specimens may bear as many as 200 flowers, with pink sepals and orange-red petals. This orchid requires growing conditions in the warm house, where it should be given full light for most of the year, combined with a high humidity. Under these circumstances it will bloom freely. Continual overhead spraying is an advantage, when long trailing aerial roots will develop readily. Basket culture suits this orchid, when it can be hung close to the glass for maximum light, with room for its hanging roots.

There is a tremendous variety of colours to be found among the hybrids from *Vanda sanderana,* and the tessellated markings on the lower sepals are equally varied. Vanda flowers open small and rather colourless; as the flowers mature over a few days they grow larger and their colour intensifies. 140♦

A cross between *V.* Emma Van Deventer and *V. sanderana,* this has become a very popular hybrid for the collector because it generally blooms twice a year, in spring and early autumn. The flowers, produced abundantly, are pink with purplish-brown markings.

All vanda hybrids should be well fed during most of the year. Owing to the high temperatures and humidity, which are important factors in their culture, they can take more artificial feeding than most orchids, providing there is a good healthy aerial root system. Regular overhead spraying is also important to prevent dehydration of the foliage, which can quickly occur in dry conditions. Once vanda leaves have been allowed to shrivel and have become limp, it can be a long and difficult task to encourage them to regain their vigour. Vandas do well only in heated, sunny greenhouses and should not be attempted as houseplants. They are not good subjects for people who are just starting to grow orchids. 141♦

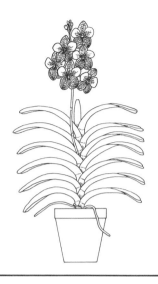 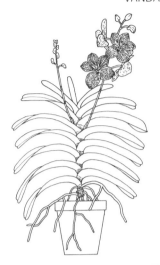

Vanda Onomea 'Walcrest'

- Warm: 18°C (65°F)
- A challenge to grow
- Summer flowering
- Evergreen/no rest

This hybrid between *V. Rothschildiana* and *V. sanderana* has proved a robust plant for warm conditions, producing many flowers of pink patterned with reddish-mauve, up to 15cm (6in) across. It grows freely and, although it normally flowers in summer, may bloom twice a year.

In Thailand, where these beautiful orchids can be grown with extreme ease, they are produced as cut flowers, which find a ready market all over the world. These hybrids come in many fine colours and have become extremely popular.

Bud drop is a problem that can occur in vandas rather more so than with other orchids. The problem is usually caused by insufficient light being available to the plants, combined with summer temperatures at their minimum.

The successful flowering of vandas relies to a great extent on the immediate outside weather conditions and the time of year. 139♦

Vanda Rothschildiana

- Warm: 18°C (65°F)
- Moderately easy to grow
- Winter flowering
- Evergreen/no rest

Sometimes called a species but more often known as a hybrid, this cross between *V. coerulea* and *V. sanderana* is a display of nature at its finest. The plant has 25cm (10in) leaves, and grows to a height of about 76cm (30in). The flower spikes are arching and crowded with five to ten flowers of intense blue, almost crystalline in texture. The blooms, which are flat-faced and appear in mid-winter, are often 13-15cm (5-6in) across. This remarkable orchid can carry as many as three or four spikes of flowers.

Blue is an extremely rare colour in orchids and therefore any blue orchid carries a special appeal to growers. *Vanda* Rothschildiana is one of the finest deep blue orchids in the world. Being a robust grower, it is somewhat easier than many other hybrids and a good plant for a vanda fancier to start with. However, it requires warm and sunny conditions with a high humidity at all times. *V.* Rothschildiana was first raised in 1931, since when the cross has been remade many times. 142♦

Vanda sanderana
- Warm: 18°C (65°F)
- A challenge to grow
- Summer flowering
- Evergreen/semi-rest

Vanda suavis
- Warm: 18°C (65°F)
- Moderately easy to grow
- Autumn/winter flowering
- Evergreen/semi-rest

A magnificent summer-flowering orchid from the Philippines that grows to about 60cm (2ft) or more in height. The leaves are 30-38cm (12-15in) long, and the flower spikes semi-erect with seven to 20 flowers clustered together. The flowers, 13cm (5in) across, are almost flat, with the upper sepal soft rose to white in colour suffused with whitish-pink, and the lower sepals round, slightly larger, and tawny yellow crossed with red markings. The petals are smaller than the sepals and are white to rose coloured with red blotches near the base; the lip is tawny yellow, streaked with red. Although this species adjusts to varying conditions and will, if necessary, tolerate some coolness, it generally grows best in warmth and sun.

This species has been used extensively for the breeding of quality hybrids and is in the pedigree of most modern *Vanda* hybrids. However, the species is today quite rare and is seldom seen in cultivation in the western world.141♦

Coming from Java and Bali, this free-flowering strap-leaved epiphyte bears colourful flowers in autumn and early winter. The stems are densely leafy with curving leaves about 25cm (10in) long and 2.5cm (1in) wide. Flower spikes are horizontal, shorter than the leaves and carry five to ten flowers that vary in shape and colour. Typically they have whitish-yellow sepals and petals barred or spotted with red-brown, usually flushed with pale magenta near the base. The fragrant waxy flowers are about 7.5cm (3in) across. This vanda is moderately easy to coax into bloom in warm sunny conditions, although it should not be attempted by beginners. A well-grown plant can reach to a considerable height and in full leaf is a grand sight. It is also found under the name of *Vanda tricolor*.

Unobtainable from the wild, the few plants in cultivation are usually the result of propagating existing stock. New plants, complete with roots, are occasionally formed around the base of the parent. 143♦

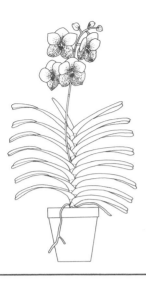

Vanda Thonglor

- Warm: 18°C (65°F)
- A challenge to grow
- Varied flowering season
- Evergreen/no rest

Raised in Thailand, the home of the vandas, this beautiful hybrid combines the desired qualities of full shape and exciting colour, both inherited largely from the *Vanda sanderana* influence in its background. The rounded, 6-7.5cm (2.4-3in) flowers are rose-mauve, the lower petals and sepals strikingly marked with crimson. This plant, which normally flowers in the summer but may bloom at any season, should be grown in warm conditions.

Vandas should be grown in a warm, sunny greenhouse that is adapted to their special needs. These are a combination of warmth, light and humidity. When successfully grown a modest collection will produce flowers for most of the year, which is one of the most appealing attributes of these beautiful orchids. Unless adequate heat and light can be given them, they should not be attempted. They are a specialist's orchid and are not suited to the beginner, the exception being *Vanda cristata*. 142♦

Vuylstekeara Cambria 'Plush'

- Cool/warm: 10-16°C (50-60°F)
- Easy to grow and flower
- Varied flowering season
- Evergreen/no rest

Every now and again a classic hybrid appears on the scene and *Vuylstekeara* Cambria 'Plush' is surely one of these. Although the cross was made in 1931, it was not until 1967 that the variety 'Plush' received a First Class Certificate from the Royal Horticultural Society, and 1973 when it obtained a First Class Certificate from the American Orchid Society – a unique double for a unique clone. Vuylstekearas are produced by introducing *Miltonia* (the pansy orchids) into *Odontioda* breeding, and they are characterized by large miltonia-type lips and glowing colours. This plant has 9cm (3.5in) dark red flowers, with large red and white lips.

Adaptability to various growing conditions has helped to make Cambria popular throughout the world; it is ideal for almost all collections, because it will grow well in cool, intermediate or warm environments. It also makes an ideal beginner's houseplant; the charming flowers never fail to please everyone. 144♦

Wilsonara Widecombe Fair

- Cool/intermediate: 10-13°C (50-55°F)
- Easy to grow and flower
- Varied flowering season
- Evergreen/no rest

This hybrid between the small but many-flowered species *Oncidium incurvum* and *Odontioda* Florence Stirling produces long spikes and many 5cm (2in) white flowers, which are heavily marked with pink, and is well suited for the mixed collection. The plant can be grown in cool or intermediate conditions, and will tolerate fluctuations in temperature.

Although the individual flowers are smaller and more 'starry' than most intergeneric odontoglossums, they are uniquely pretty and when massed on the huge branching 'Christmas tree' flower spikes are quite breath-taking. This hybrid represents a different breeding line, characterized by the species *Oncidium incurvum*, which has dominated the size and shape of the individual flowers as well as the flowering habit. It is an unusual and charming addition to any collection. Its adaptability and ease of culture make it an ideal beginner's orchid.

It should be kept moist all year and lightly sprayed in summer. 144♦

Zygopetalum intermedium

- Intermediate: 13°C (55°F)
- Moderately easy to grow
- Winter flowering
- Evergreen/dry rest

This genus comprises 20 species, most of which come from Brazil. They are mainly terrestrial, producing rounded pseudobulbs with long but fairly narrow leaves.

These are plants for the intermediate house and require good light, with plenty of moisture at the root when in full growth. Air movement around the plant in conditions of high humidity is very important, otherwise the leaves soon become badly spotted; and, for this reason, they should never be sprayed.

Often known as *Z. mackayi*, this plant produces an upright flower spike, 46-60cm (18-24in) in height, from inside the first leaves of a new growth. The spike bears four to eight flowers, each 7.5cm (3in) across. The sepals and petals are of equal size, and bright green blotched with brown. The lip, in contrast, is broad, flat and basically white, heavily lined with purple. These heavily scented flowers last for four or five weeks during the winter months. 144♦

Further Reading

Birk, L.A., *Growing Cymbidium Orchids at Home,* L.A. Birk, California, 1977.

Blowers, J.W., *Pictorial Orchid Growing,* J.W. Blowers, Maidstone, 1966.

Bowen, L., *The Art and Craft of Growing Orchids,* Batsford, London, 1976.

Cohen, B. and Roberts, E., *Growing Orchids in the Home,* Hodder and Stoughton, London, 1975.

Curtis, C.H., *Orchids – Their description and Cultivation,* Putnam, London, 1950.

Dodson, C.H. and Gillespie, R.J., *The Biology of the Orchids,* Mid-America Orchid Congress, Tennessee, 1967.

Freed, H., *Orchids and Serendipity,* Prentice-Hall, New York and London, 1970.

Hawkes, A.D., *Encyclopedia of Cultivated Orchids,* Faber & Faber, London, 1965.

Kramer, J., *Growing Orchids at your Windows,* D. van Nostrand, New York, 1963.

Kramer, J., *Orchids: Flowers of Romance and Mystery,* Harry N. Abrams, New York, 1975.

Nicholls, W.H., *Orchids of Australia,* Thomas Nelson, Sydney, Australia, 1969.

Noble, M., *You Can Grow Orchids,* M. Noble, Florida, 1964.

Northern, R.T., *Orchids as House Plants,* Dover Publications, New York, 1955.

Northern, R.T., *Home Orchid Growing,* Van Nostrand Reinhold, New York, 1970.

The Orchid Stud Book, Hurst & Rolfe, London, 1909.

Paul, M., *Orchids – Care and Growth,* Merlin Press, London, 1964.

Richter, W., *Orchid Care: A Guide to Cultivation and Breeding,* Macmillan, London, 1969.

Rittershausen, P.R.C., *Successful Orchid Culture,* Collingridge, London, 1953.

Rittershausen, B. and Rittershausen, W., *Popular Orchids,* Stockwell, Devon, 1970.

Rittershausen, B. and Rittershausen, W., *Orchids – in Colour,* Blandford, Dorset, 1979.

Sander, D.F., *Orchids and their Cultivation,* Blandford, London, 1962.

Sanders' Complete List of Orchid Hybrids, Royal Horticultural Society, London, 1966, available from the American Orchid Society, Cambridge, Massachusetts.

Sessler, G.J., *Orchids – and how to grow them,* Prentice-Hall, New York and London, 1978.

Skelsey, A., *The Time-Life Encyclopedia of Gardening: Orchids,* Time-Life Books, Virginia, 1978.

Sunset Books, *How to Grow Orchids,* Lane, California, 1977.

Swinson, A., *Frederick Sander: The Orchid King,* Hodder and Stoughton, London, 1970

Thompson, P.A., *Orchids from Seed,* Royal Botanic Gardens, Kew, 1977.

Williams, B.S., *Orchid Growers' Manual,* Wheldon and Wesley, Herts, 1894; reprint Hafner, Connecticut, 1961.

Veitch, J. and Sons, *Manual of Orchidaceous Plants,* H.M. Pollett, London, 1887.

Journals

American Orchid Society Bulletin, American Orchid Society, Cambridge, Massachusetts, USA.

Australian Orchid Review, The Australian Orchid Council, Sydney, Australia.

Die Orchidee, Deutsche Orchideen-Gesellschaft, Frankfurt, West Germany.

Orchids In New Zealand, the New Zealand Orchid Society, Wellington, New Zealand.

The Orchid Digest, The Orchid Digest Corporation, Orinda, California, USA.

The Orchid Review, The Orchid Review, Ltd., Kingsteignton, Newton Abbot, Devon, England.

The South African Orchid Journal, the South African Orchid Council, University of Natal, South Africa.

Useful Terms

Words in *italics* refer to separate entries within the list.

Adj. = Adjective
Cf. = Compare
Pl. = Plural

Adventitious Usually applied to roots, or any growth produced from a site other than the usual or normal.

Aerial Living without contact with compost or the ground.

Anther The part of the *stamen* containing *pollen.*

Anther cap The cap covering the *pollen* masses.

Articulate Jointed; possessing a *node* or joint.

Axil The upper angle between a stem or branch and a leaf.

Back bulb Old *pseudobulb,* usually without leaves.

Bifoliate Having two leaves.

Bigeneric Involving two *genera* in the parentage of a plant.

Bisexual Two sexed, the flowers possessing both *stamens* and *pistils.* (cf. *unisexual*).

Bract A reduced leaf-like organ protecting a flower stalk.

Bulbous Having the character of a bulb.

Calceolate Slipper-shaped.

Callus The protective tissue covering a cut or bruised surface.

Chlorophyll The green pigment in plants, essential for the manufacture of food.

Chlorotic Excessive yellowing due to a breaking down of the *chlorophyll.*

Chromosome A structure within the cell nucleus, which carries the *genes.*

Clone An individual plant raised from a single seed, and all its subsequent *vegetative propagations.*

Column The central body of the orchid flower formed by the union of the *stamens* and *pistil.*

Crest A raised, fringed or toothed ridge found on the *lip.*

Cross-pollinate The *pollination* of one flower with the *pollen* from another flower. (cf. *self-pollination*).

Cultivar An individual plant in cultivation, including its *vegetative propagations.*

Deciduous Losing leaves at the end of the growing season.

Diploid Having the normal complement of a double set of *chromosomes.*

Division The means by which a single *cultivar* is divided into two or more plants.

Dorsal Pertaining to the back or outer surface. (cf. *ventral*).

Endemic Occurring only in a given area, and not elsewhere.

Epiphyte A plant that grows on another plant but is not a *parasite,* as it obtains nourishment from the air.

Family A group of related *genera.*

Filiform Long, slender or thread like.

Fimbriate Fringed.

Gene The unit of inheritance, located at a specific site on a *chromosome.*

Genus A subdivision of a *family,* consisting of one or more *species* which show similar characteristics and appear to have a common ancestry. Adj. generic. Pl. genera.

Grex A group, applied collectively to the progeny of a given cross between two plants.

Habitat The locality in which a plant normally grows.

Hirsute *Pubescent,* the hairs being coarse and stiff.

Hybrid The offspring resulting from the cross between two different *species* or hybrids.

Inbreeding *Self-pollinating.*

Inflorescence The flowering part of a plant.

Intergeneric Between or among two or more *genera*.

Internode The part of a stem between two *nodes*.

Keel A projecting ridge.

Keiki A plantlet produced as an offset or offshoot from another plant. (A Hawaiian term used by orchidists.)

Labellum The *lip,* or modified *petal* of an orchid flower.

Lateral Of or pertaining to the side of an organ. (cf. *terminal*).

Lead A new *vegetative* growth.

Linear Long and narrow, with parallel margins.

Lip The *labellum,* usually quite distinct from the other two *petals.*

Lithophyte A plant which grows on rocks. Adj. lithophytic.

Mericlone A plant produced by *meristem* culture.

Meristem *Vegetative propagation* of plants by cultivating new shoot tissue under special laboratory conditions.

Monofoliate Having only one leaf.

Monopodial Growing only from the apex of the plant.

Mutation A departure from the parent type; a *sport.*

Natural hybrid A *hybrid* produced by chance in the wild.

Nectary A gland or secreting organ that produces nectar.

Node A joint on a stem.

Ovary The central female part of a flower.

Parasite A plant that lives on and derives part or all of its nourishment from another plant. Adj. parasitic. (cf. *epiphyte.*

Pendulous Hanging downwards, or inclined.

Petal One of the three inner segments of an orchid flower, which is not modified to form the *lip.*

Pistil The seed-bearing organ of a flower consisting of the *ovary, stigma* and *style.*

Plicate Pleated, or folded like a fan.

Pollen The fertilizing grains borne by the *anther.*

Pollination The transfer of *pollen* from the anther to the *stigma.*

Pollinia The masses of pollen grains found in the *anther.*

Polyploid Containing one or more additional sets of *chromosomes* beyond the normal *diploid* number.

Proliferation Offshoots; the growth of buds that normally remain dormant.

Protocorm A tuber-like structure formed in the early stages of a plant's development.

Pseudobulb The thickened portion of a stem, but not a true bulb.

Pubescent Covered with fine hairs or down.

Quadrigeneric Pertaining to four *genera.*

Raceme A simple *inflorescence* of stalked flowers.

Recurved Curved downwards or backwards.

Rhizome A root-bearing horizontal stem, which, in orchids, usually lies on or just beneath the ground surface.

Saccate Pouched, or bag-like.

Saprophyte A plant which lives on dead organic matter. Adj. saprophytic.

Scape A flower stalk without leaves, arising directly from the ground.

Self-pollination The *pollination* of a flower by its own *pollen.* (cf. *cross-pollination*).

Semiterete Semicircular in cross-section; semicylindrical. (cf. *terete*).

Sepal One of the three outer segments of an orchid flower.

Sheath A tubular envelope protecting the developing *inflorescence*.

Species A group of plants sharing one or more common characteristics which make it distinct from any other group. Adj. specific.

Spike A flower stem.

Sport A deviation from the usual form; a *mutation*.

Spur A hollow tubular extension of the *lip*.

Stamen The male organ of a flower, bearing the *pollen*.

Style The part of the *pistil* bearing the *stigma*.

Symbiosis The close association of dissimilar organisms, with benefit to both. Adj. symbiotic.

Sympodial A form of growth in which each new shoot, arising from the *rhizome* of the previous growth, is a complete plant.

Synonym A surplus name, arising when a *species* has been given two or more names.

Terete Circular in cross-section; cylindrical (cf. *semiterete*).

Terminal At the end of the axis (cf. *lateral*).

Terrestrial Growing in or on the ground.

Tribe A group of related *genera*.

Trigeneric Pertaining to three *genera*.

Tuber A thickened, normally underground stem.

Unifoliate With one leaf.

Unilateral Arranged only on one side.

Unisexual Having flowers of one sex only. (cf. *bisexual*).

Variety A subdivision of a *species*; a group of plants that differ slightly from the main *species type*.

Vegetative propagation The increasing of a particular plant by *division*, or by *meristem* culture.

Velamen The thick layer of cells covering the roots of *epiphytic* orchids.

Ventral The front (cf. *dorsal*).

Verrucose Covered with wart-like projections.

Picture Credits

The publishers with to thank the following photographers and agencies who have supplied photographs for this book. Photographs have been credited by page number and position on the page: (B) bottom, (T) Top, (C) Centre, (BL) Bottom left, etc.

A-Z Botanical Collection: 16
Alec Bristow: 40(TR), 45(B)
Eric Crichton: Endpapers, Title page, 8(T), 9, 10, 11, 12, 13, 14, 15, 33(BL,BR), 34, 35(T), 36, 37, 38, 39, 41, 42(T), 43(TR,BR), 44, 46, 47, 48, 65, 66(TL,B), 67(T), 68(B), 69, 70(TR), 71, 72, 73, 74, 75, 76, 77, 78(TR,B), 79, 80, 97, 98, 99, 100, 101, 102, 103, 104, 105, 106, 107, 108, 109, 110, 111, 112, 129, 130, 131, 132, 133, 134(TL), 135, 136, 137, 138, 142, 143, 144
Alan Greatwood: 8(B), 35(BL,BR), 42(B), 66(TR), 67(BR), 68(TL), 70(TL,B), 78(TL), 134(BL)
Charles Marden Fitch: 140
J.R. Oddy: 141(BR)
Orchid Society of Great Britain: 40(TL)
Herman Pigors: 139, 141(TR)
Gerald Rodway: 33(T), 40(B), 45(TR)

PRINTED IN BELGIUM BY

proost
INTERNATIONAL BOOK PRODUCTION

Paphiopedilum insigne